In Praise of Dancing at the Crossroads

"Lorna Czarnota has developed theories, stories and activities for professionals that have been used by me for several years with great success. The step by step outlines for group work in the Practitioners Guide have proven invaluable to me."

Susan McCullough, M.A., M.Ed.
National Board Certified School Counselor (U.S.)
School Counselor, Leipzig International School
Leipzig, Germany

"Lorna is a dedicated storyteller who has the gift of reaching through the barriers and touching the core of young people of all ages. Her stories present opportunities for the listener (reader) to show empathy, identify and personalize situations and look for universal truths. I have seen her touch the most resistant adolescent in crisis and provide food for thought. Lorna's stories offer a banquet for the soul."

Sylvia H. Nadler, Executive Director of Compass House
(Shelter for Runaway and Homeless Youth)
Buffalo, New York

"At-risk youth have often lived through hard times and trauma. Many of them react to probation officers, counselors, and social workers by closing up, communicating only minimally. Stories, unlike conventional helping methods, enter the brain "sideways," and youth can use stories to grapple with issues of identity and meaning. Lorna MacDonald Czarnota's skill as a master storyteller and her fifteen years of experience in working with at-risk youth have produced a valuable resource."

James Winship, MSW, Ph.D.
Professor and Chair of Social Work at the University of Wisconsin-Whitewater
Former director of Youth Services at a settlement house.

"Here in Ireland we are aware of Lorna Czarnota's excellent work with at-risk youth and their families and also in detention centers and shelters. She demonstrates how the power of storytelling can reach those young people who are most vulnerable and give them the confidence to rebuild lives which have been shattered by events which are often outside their control. Dancing at the Crossroads will prove a valuable tool for storytellers everywhere."

Liz Weir, Storyteller
Recipient of the International Storybridge Award
Cushendall, Ireland

"Whether you are a provider of emotional support to another, a person in need of guidance, or someone who just wants to understand the power of story, Lorna's thoughtful, sensitive guide won't disappoint you. Long overdue in the field of healing story, Lorna's deep research and thoughtful application of story provides what so many of us have been waiting for to guide us forward."

Lani Peterson, Psy.D.
Co-chair, Healing Story Alliance
Andover MA.

"Lorna's writings are inspirational as well as thoughtful, and full of useful approaches to the challenges of facing difficult situations and mobilizing the energies needed to achieve desired goals. Lorna's books are packed with good advice, reference material, and a true sense of humanness. Colleges and educational opportunity centers should consider Lorna's writings as guideposts for working effectively with the kind of wounded but motivated people that we encounter and serve."

Mike Seliger, PhD
Bronx Community College Dean
Executive Committee Healing Story Alliance.

"The stories, methods and ideas Lorna Czarnota has compiled in Dancing at the Crossroads will help parents of adolescents learn to communicate with, accept and mentor them through the difficult teens years."

Lynn Kratz Ryan, Parent of three
Grand Island, New York

"It is Lorna's caring heart that defines her work and her life. In her storytelling, writing, and workshop facilitating, her heart speaks in ways that encourage us to live, love, and learn, always with open minds and open hearts. She is an award-winning, degreed professional who allows neither accolades nor academe to interfere with the very delicate work of empowering people, especially at-risk teens."

Karima Amin, Storyteller, Author, Activist
Buffalo, New York.

"This body of work by Lorna Czarnota, compiled over fifteen years in practice using story to reach at-risk youth, is a long time coming and will prove invaluable to caregivers, practitioners and storytellers. Lorna includes everything that might be needed to work one-on-one or with groups of youth, and has taken great care to focus on compassion and understanding in her work with this population."

Allison M. Cox, MA Counseling Psychology
Graduate Certificate in Public Health
co-editor and contributor to the Healing Heart books.
State of Washington

Dancing at the Crossroads

2015

Other Books by Lorna MacDonald Czarnota

Medieval Tales that Kids Can Read and Tell

Legends, Lore and Secrets of Western New York

Wicked Niagara: the Sinister Side of the Niagara Frontier Breadline Blue

Dancing at the Crossroads: Stories and Activities for At-Risk Youth Programming

Dancing at the Crossroads: A Guide for Practitioners in At-Risk Youth Programming

American and Pioneer Sites of Upstate New York: Westward Trails From Albany to Buffalo

Audio Recordings

Crossroads: Stories of Choice and Empowerment

Dancing in Dark Waters

Dancing at the Crossroads

A Guide for Caregivers in At-Risk Youth Programming

Lorna MacDonald Czarnota

with collaborations by Diana Koch

Parkhurst Brothers Publishers
MARION • MICHIGAN

Dancing at the Crossroads: A Guide for Caregivers in At-Risk Youth Programming

www.parkhurstbrothers.com

Parkhurst Brothers books are distributed to the trade through the Chicago Distribution Center, and may be ordered through Ingram Book Company, Baker & Taylor, Follett Library Resources and other book industry wholesalers. To order from Chicago Distribution Center, phone 1-800-621-2736 or send a fax to 800-621-8476. Copies of this and other Parkhurst Brothers Inc., Publishers titles are available to organizations and corporations for purchase in quantity by contacting Special Sales Department at our home office location, listed on our web site. Manuscript submission guidelines for this publishing company are available at our web site.

Printed in the United States of America

First Edition, 2014
2018 2017 2016 2015 2014 10 9 8 7 6 5 4 3 2 1

ISBN: Trade Paperback 9781624910364

Cataloging in Publication Data will be available on the publisher's website

Edited, Cover and Page Design by: MyLinda Butterworth
Acquired for Parkhurst Brothers Inc., Publishers by: Ted Parkhurst

This book is printed on archival-quality paper that meets requirements of the American National Standard for Information Sciences, Permanence of Paper, Printed Library Materials, ANSI Z39.48-1984.

To Lynn Ryan, Darcie, and Emily S.
I wrote this book for you. You are never alone in the dark places and I dance with you in the light.

Acknowledgments

Thank you to the many people who helped with and supported this work.

To my publisher Ted Parkhurst for bringing this important work to fruition and to editor and book-designer MyLinda Butterworth for her attention to detail.

Diana Koch, for collaborating on the clinical portions of this project, and for her constant friendship, support, and mentorship.

Sylvia Nadler of Compass House, Mark O'Brien, formerly of Hopevale Incorporated, and Sister Janet of TRY house. Your work with at-risk youth inspired me and what I have learned from you is priceless.

Dan Keding for consenting the use of his original the Two Warriors.

To the early readers who gave feedback on my programs, you are so important to this work. Susan McCullough, Lani Peterson, Maya Opavska, and Karima Amin. A special thank you toSusan Klein, a wonderful storyteller and mentor, for her suggestions on placement of some stories and chapters in this book.

Laura Simms for consenting the use of her story "The Black Prince."

My loving life partner, Thomas Heim, without whose support I could not even do my work, and my niece Charisse, who taught me how to love unconditionally.

My parents, David and Mary MacDonald whose love of children inspired me, and who taught me about the world. You are missed more than you could know. I know you would have been proud to hold this book in your hands.

Contents

Foreword

Our culture is suffering a crisis. Many children are victims of broken and abusive homes and a lack of supervision. Busing children from neighborhood schools to unfamiliar facilities has made it impossible for community leaders such as shopkeepers and neighbors to maintain visual contact with them. Televisions talk at the children but cannot give the feedback that children need and crave. Many families are so scattered in their activities that they do not eat dinner together, a time that used to be reserved for catching up on the family's interests and stories. As a result, family ritual has been diluted or is nonexistent in many homes. The tragic outcomes of these absences are a crumbling foundation and a sketchy portrait of expectation, moral value, and hope for future success. Many children have become lost. The children who survive are those who have family or other caring adult support.

Today's teens face more than their parents ever imagined. Rebellion is nothing new, nor is violence, but the enormity and rate are greater than ever before. In our parents' day, people worried about getting work, infectious disease, and keeping their daughters from having premarital sex. Those concerns are still present but they are coupled with more troubling problems.

Little thought was given to whether a child might be shot walking to and from school or in school for that matter. Our parents didn't worry as much about whether we would be tempted to try drugs, let alone possibly die from an overdose of pills found in their own medicine cabinets. Parents seldom thought about children going to prison for theft, violence, or murder. They gave little thought about their daughters being raped and molested, or their sons for that matter. Guns were for hunting and children didn't hide them in their book bags. Then again, our parents and grandparents usually had supportive, strict, but loving parents to raise them. A child seldom returned from school to an empty house.

Today, hardly a day goes by that we do not hear about the tragic death of a youth, either by suicide or at the hands of another child. Many children have only one parent to care for them. Sometimes that parent finds it necessary to work outside the home in order to provide, leaving children to fend for themselves much of the time. Even the adults responsible for children find themselves at odds rather than in partnership with each other.

The times have changed but the needs remain the same. Children need and want supervision on their journey to becoming adults. It is time to make a change in our way of mentoring and work together again.

It is my hope that the stories in this book will inspire you, that the knowledge shared here will fortify your personal strength to maintain contact and connection with the young people in your life, and the years of collected, tried and tested programs will make your journey into youth mentoring easier. We are all part of this great dance at the crossroads. The ground is well worn but not without its bumps. We cannot afford to let our young people down. So, let's dance!

LMC

Preface

Welcome to the Crossroads, the place where we dance when we experience changes in our lives. The Crossroads is a place of wildness, but it is here we can be remade.

This book is written to offer parents, grandparents, teachers, ministers, counselors, storytellers and other caregivers a unique way to reach and motivate at-risk youth, and the support they need for their own roles in these relationships. The author hopes that it encourages all adults to find ways of taking part in the lives of young people, to mentor and partner with youth for a brighter future. Our teens will be grown in a very short time and we need to take responsibility for them, whether they are our own children or our community's children. Looking at them, we see ourselves.

This book is a comprehensive guide containing knowledge collected over fifteen years of working with at-risk youth through story, reading, and conversation with therapists and social workers. This book contains theories and stories created, designed, and tested by the author in support of youth and those who care for them. This information is applicable to both boys and girls, as well as adult trauma survivors. Additional stories, activities, workshops, and curriculums may be found in *Dancing at the Crossroads: Stories and Activities.*

The author's adaptations of traditional stories are included in their entirety for the reader's convenience. Stories that other tellers have written, adapted, or are already published are given in synopsis form with the sources cited, unless the storyteller gave permission to print the whole story. Every effort has been made to credit sources.

Diana Koch, a colleague and certified social worker, has collaborated on portions of this book, and her comments and observations are noted.

Introduction: The Community of Story

THE ART OF STORYTELLING has made an increasing appearance in schools and libraries over the past four decades. Before the modern movement began in the 1970s, few children in the United States knew about storytelling, and this continued throughout the 1980s in many places. But ask any child today and most will say they have heard a teller at least once. At the beginning of the 21st century, the public at-large still remains mostly unfamiliar with storytelling as a community activity. Storytelling continues to be considered something only for children and entertainment, when in fact in older societies, the storyteller was a revered member of the community, a wise one who had the answers to many questions. Stories were considered entertaining, but they were and are a wellspring of information about the roles people play, the rules of society, the morals and values of the community, and the history of the tribe or nation. Stories are academically instructional. The storyteller of old was inseparable from the story, and the story inseparable from the community. Although the role of teller and tale may be different today, stories really have always been models for living.

Many stories have hidden meanings and messages, comprehended only by initiates as inside jokes. Long ago, whole communities, from the oldest member to the youngest, huddled together to hear these tales. Likely, there were no children's or adult stories per se. Perhaps all stories held equal weight and were appreciated in different ways depending on the listener's perception and "inside" knowledge.

Creating that kind of community today is much more difficult. While mass communications has shrunk our world, we typically live farther from our birthplaces and family homes than people in older societies did. We are more isolated from physical community than ever before. We can read and hear about, or watch events unfold live on television or radio, and send e-mail or social network messages to people we have never met, all without any face-to-face interaction or consequence. This may be why it is vastly refreshing to sit close to others, enjoying the sound of each other's breath and sharing each other's anxiety, excitement, and relief when hearing a tale told live. Teens are no exception. They feel comforted by the simplicity of the act of storytelling and special because an adult has shared something incredibly beautiful without any strings attached.

Something wonderful happens when a story is told within a group of people. Listeners feel as if the story is just for them, and at the same time the story becomes part of that group's collective shared experience. This helps form community, a shared identity with two or more people.

The Growing Circle

written by Lorna MacDonald Czarnota

Shuffling and soft singing woke Dominique in the middle of the night. She followed the long line of women. She watched them take their places among the ancient rocks and trees.

-Dominique-

Her whispered name hung in the air. It oozed like sap from the trees. It felt like soft rain on her face.

Dominique entered the clearing and sat at their feet. She did not know why they called her, but she liked their stories.

It was quiet. The only sound came from the peepers beyond the firelight. Dominique's voice was loud when she spoke.

"Tell me a story."

"You're too little."

"Too young."

"Come back when you're older."

Dominique was eleven, when the sun came up she would be twelve. She felt old enough, and asked, "How can I grow without the stories?"

It was the right question. The women smiled.

Auntie Esther, who always smelled musty, replied, "I'll tell you a story."

Dominique plugged her nose as her aunt removed her shoe. Esther's foot was green. Her toes were crusted like moldy bread and Dominique didn't want to look. Her aunt motioned her closer.

The green mold was really a whole forest of trees. There were mountains, and streams, and tiny creatures moving in and out and around Esther's toes.

Auntie Esther pulled a leaf from deep inside her shoe. She cupped it in her hand.

In a whisper, so the rocks would not hear, she said, "This is the secret of life."

"A leaf?" asked Dominique.

"Not just any leaf," replied Auntie Esther. "This is from the first tree I planted when I was your age."

Auntie Esther handed the leaf to Dominique.

"We are the ones who make things grow."

"Ha ha ha!" Laughter filled the clearing.

Auntie Connie was Dominique's youngest aunt. She was round and full with beaded cornrow braids that hung to her shoulders. Her laugh was wonderful.

"I'll show you something."

She leaned forward, hands on her knees. Her eyes turned upward. The braids moved. They wriggled and stood straight out from Connie's head. The braids were snakes that danced and twisted back and forth with beaded collars.

Auntie Connie pulled a l-o-o-o-ng living braid from her hair.

"*This* is the secret of life."

"I thought the secret was a leaf," Dominique said.

"So is this," said Auntie Connie. "This snake will grow until it's too big for its skin."

Dominique sighed, "Like me."

"And then it gets a new skin. You wait and see if you do too." Auntie Connie smiled. Dominique always liked her smile.

Each woman told a story.

"We are culture keepers."

"We sing to the world."

"We bring new life."

"And this is our secret."

Dominique promised to keep the secret until it was time to tell her own story. She felt more grown up.

But one woman had not told her story. She sat in shadow and silence. This woman was the oldest of them all. She smelled like the earth, and the trees, and the snows, and the mountain streams. Her voice was like the rustling wind. It whispered like a new morning. Around her shoulders hung a long shawl. Its fringe lightly brushed the earth.

"Grandmother, you have not told your story yet," said Dominique. "Where is it?"

Grandmother's eyes shone as Dominique came closer. Silver light seeped through the opening of her shawl. Slowly, *very slowly*, Grandmother unfolded it.

The shadows evaporated. For the first time, Dominique saw other excited young faces just outside the circle. But, *this* was Dominique's night. She was drawn to Grandmother, who was bathed in silver light. It swirled about her head and feet. The light spilled from a large basket on Grandmother's lap and wrapped around Dominique.

"This is my secret," said Grandmother. "I keep light and I hold the stories."

The basket held Auntie Connie's snakes and Auntie Esther's trees. Dominique saw all the stories she had heard in her young life, and more. A feeling of hope surrounded her.

Grandmother took a silver thread from the basket and pressed it into Dominique's hand. She wrapped the shawl around the basket and the shadows returned.

"I can't see it," said Dominique. "I want to see more."

Grandmother smiled.

"You can't see it *all* today, but it is there and always will be." Grandmother placed a hand on Dominique's shoulder. "Now you have what you need to weave a basket for your stories."

Dominique looked at the silver thread that glowed brightly in her hand. She knew she was welcome with the other girls at the edge of the growing circle. Someday she would take her place among the ancient trees and rocks. Someday Dominique would tell her own story.

Community and Our Youth

Community may not understand the key role it can play in a child's life, but there is good news. Our understanding of children is changing. We are beginning to realize that they have to build skills. Their parents and their communities teach those skills. Communities and adults in their church might take time to get to know them or involve them in a community project. A child's future can be made if the community recognizes that child as a valuable part of the whole and supports that child as a future contributing adult.

Among abused or neglected teens, it is often when someone in the community "took the time to see the light in them" that made the difference. When community ignores these youth, they may develop conduct disorders and continue to struggle with the effects of abuse or neglect into adulthood. Mentored children can connect to people and learn to care. They develop empathy and a sense of responsibility because someone saw their potential. Without this support, the child may become an adult with multiple problems and an inability to solve them on their own.

"Helping people is helping them acclimate." Judith Herman, *Trauma and Recovery*, (1992) Perseus Books.

The community is important to children who come from connected families as well. Youth need people outside the family who see that they have special skills and talents. The 40 Developmental Assets from the Search Institute of Minneapolis, MN, are a foundation for these skills in a variety of areas, including social skills, connection, responsibility,

> support, volunteering, arts, school, and daily living. These skills enable children to cope with everyday events toward a successful and effective life. Many of these assets are focused on community. They highlight those things a young person might do well such as volunteering, hobbies, crafts, and projects that can be seen from beginning to end. They help boost self-esteem. Acceptance by the community can lead to the desire to take care of the community. In unconnected families, community plays an even more important role. For these children, the community becomes an extended family.
>
> There was a time when parents knew about anything their child had done wrong and a parent was waiting for that child when they got home from school. There was something unnerving about your mother waiting at the door and that look of disappointment on her face that made you think twice about getting into trouble. Today, we are lucky if a teacher calls from school or the neighbor lets us know what happened down the street. Accountability must go beyond the door of our homes and our schools. This makes our children better people and reassures parents that their children are not alone out there. They are part of a greater whole.
>
> *Diana Koch*

A boy dropped a paper cup on my lawn. He would have left it there and kept on walking, but I saw him from my porch.

"I saw that," I said.

He replied "What?"

"You dropped that cup."

"F.U.," he replied.

"You need to pick it up," I said.

He did pick up the cup. He knew I was not going away and perhaps part of him realized my lawn was his lawn. That is an important concept in today's growing world. Children need to know we are watching.

> My father was stationed in Europe an hour outside where my mother grew up, in a valley and small hamlet. I had the job every morning of going to the baker to get fresh rolls. My grandmother gave me her special basket with hand-embroidered linens inside for the baker to cover the rolls. All the people along the way knew who I was and said hello. The baker talked to me and gave me a treat to eat on the way home. I remember that sense of community. The neighbors all knew it was my job and expected to see me. They would acknowledge me and I felt really special. It made a difference.
> *Diana Koch*

Sending our children into the community should be like a relay race. We hand the child from one caregiver to another until the race is run and each makes sure the child makes it to the end safely. This is equally true of how we view teens. We cannot be afraid of them. We must make eye contact and engage them because they need us to do so. They may not admit it, but they also want us to include them in the community while giving them space to explore it their own way.

Children, who have been removed from their communities, either because they are incarcerated or separated from family in another way, still need a sense of belonging to a group. We will sometimes find that youth develop gang relationships for this very reason.

Diana Koch says, "Unless they are completely disconnected through pain, most young people will find a way to take whatever their environment presents to them, and create community or family. Leaders will emerge, and other young people will take the part of family siblings. The job for facility staff working with these children is to be aware and constantly create community in a healthy way. In essence, the adult staff takes on the roles of parents. This is not always easy for staff because they are in the middle of the child's struggles and healing. Environment is imperative. It needs to be safe, calm, soothing, and social."

Part I

Mentoring At-Risk Youth

Chapter 1

The Face Behind the Mask

PERSONALITY TRAITS

FORMING WORKING PARTNERSHIPS WITH YOUTH REQUIRES FLEXIBILITY, understanding, and preparation for a variety of personalities and reactions. Just as one story will not fit every teen, they also react differently to different situations. Although we should use caution when attaching labels to people, having some form of classification can help us find a place to begin the work. Teens on the street make one of two choices: to stand out or to blend in. The "blending in" and "standing out" behaviors serve different purposes. They are the masks these youth wear to protect themselves. As partners in their dance, we must not be afraid of uncovering the real self beneath the mask. The process always begins with a search for meaning.

The Chameleon Child

The chameleon can change color to blend with its surroundings. This is a survival technique used often in nature. Unlike animals in nature that have no choice regarding what they will become, people do have choices, and they sometimes choose disguise. The Chameleon Child may fall into any of three sub-categories, the Invisible Child, Stone Child, or the Diva Child.

"The Chameleon Child is a child who has learned to assess safety and sense of self by what is happening outside, rather than having a strong sense of what is going on inside. They often come from families with addiction issues where the degree of perceived threat is dependent on where the parent is in their addiction. They become adept and creative at looking at their outer world, the people who have power over them, the people they need, and how to interact with them. The goal of the Chameleon Child is to keep the other person's behaviors from escalating. They try to keep them happy and give them what they want. Many adults who came from these kinds of relationships will repeat this behavior later in work and personal relationships. Unfortunately, it sets them up for re-victimization. The youth are unaware that they are in unhealthy positions. They have not developed a good "inner place" that helps them determine whether a relationship is healthy. Their relationships are about being what the other person needs, not about equality. The Chameleon Child is a creative survivor. They lose the most because they abandon their development in order to survive. It does not benefit them to cultivate a sense of self. Physical, emotional, and psychological needs drive them to be safe and accepted. This is a serious personal loss for these children," says Koch.

"The focus in therapy for these young people is to help them build an internalized sense of self that is not entirely dependent on satisfying other people. We want them to realize that their own needs, wants, views, and opinions should be part of the relationships in which they are involved. This is one part of becoming a separate person" Koch concludes. (See "Star Woman's Basket" and "The Selkie," found in the companion book, *Dancing at the Crossroads: Stories and Activities for At-Risk Youth Programs.)*

Helping the Chameleon Child

Whether a child is hiding from danger, gaining attention, or appearing invincible, there is more to being a Chameleon Child than these behaviors. These youth need help discovering appropriate mechanisms for coping. Their number one requirement is survival. Food and shelter are basic and these youth will do anything to obtain them. They also crave affection. In desperation, they can be pressured into going against their own morals and ethics. Chameleon Children might turn to sex or drugs to get their needs met. Peers can easily push them to fit in with the crowd to achieve their goals. This may be because the Chameleon Child has a natural sense of negotiation and can read the wants of others in order to change and find acceptance. As caregivers, we need to find a way to use that skill positively.

"Our goal in therapy or storytelling," says Diana Koch, "is to discover how we can help Chameleon Children recognize that they have developed new life skills for negotiating and understanding what others need. The irony of these youth is their receptiveness to the wants and needs of others and their awareness of what drives other people. In fact, these skills are the very ones we look for in a therapist and caregiver. Balance is missing, which is what these youth need to become whole healthy people. Everything is going out, but nothing is coming back. So, the key for healing these children is helping them understand the value of what they have learned and to see it as an art.

An art or creative gift needs to be tamed. It must be worked and refined. Artists who paint need to learn those skills or their art runs rampant. They learn to control and master it. If we give children opportunities to shine in those areas and the chance to experience distress in relationships, they come to realize they can survive those moments. When we do this, we present them with a better gift than we do when we always rescue them.

Children learn that they do not have to jump into the fire all the time to survive. They can ask for things or disagree without feeling threatened.

Much of this learning can take place in interaction between helper and child negotiating together, which is why we talk about risking connection. That is the 'human' part of a relationship. A real relationship involves conflict, arguing, disagreeing, negotiating, coming together and also feeling comfortable in separation. In story, we should give the youth opportunities to see the skill of other negotiators and experience the roles of the people who receive more than they give. At-risk children need to feel comfort and pleasure with these experiences. They need to learn to feel safe enough to know they do not always have to fix things or sacrifice their individuality for acceptance." (See "The Black Prince")

The Stone Child

The Stone Child uses standing out behavior as a control measure. He or she appears strong on the outside, may be smaller in stature than peers, or is the child we classify as a bully. Stone Children seem to know which buttons to push to manipulate others, and many have strong leadership qualities.

Most often, their use of forceful behavior is how they get others to follow them. This forcefulness may be physical, sexual, emotional, or verbal. The Stone Child can be charismatic. This child is hiding behind the behavior to avoid being hurt. However, the Stone Child's standing-out behaviors also draw attention. A Stone Child is very good at blocking unwanted attention and does not form deep bonds with others. A mere facial expression seems to say, "Don't go there." The most powerful tool of Stone Children is intimidation. They guard their space.

Diana Koch says, "The Stone Child may be diagnosed with conduct disorder or antisocial personality traits. These children are the ones who have lost the most. Their sense of abandonment is so deep and solidified that sometimes there is no possibility for healing, no turning back. The future for these youth will most likely involve criminal behavior, perhaps because they have not developed empathy, accountability, or awareness of the effect they have on others. These children require our greatest effort, patience, and willingness to hold on. The child who is turned to stone is the hardest to engage.

Breaking this spell is not easy. When we do crack open the hard exterior, the person who comes out is young, untamed, and susceptible to stimulation from the outside world. He has no boundaries or buffers. Perhaps, the best way to help these youth is by engaging their strengths first. If we can see the art in their learned behaviors and respect the function of those behaviors, we can help them become smarter and find personal power. However, if we set out first to challenge those 'negative' behaviors, we give them permission to divert into the behaviors we are trying to avoid. Instead, we want to help these young people discover new skills to use in places where their old skills are not appropriate. By doing so, we teach Stone Children that they can get what they want even if it is not about survival. Our empathy toward them becomes a 'teaching moment' for empathy."

Every bully is a leader in disguise, waiting to learn the right skills.

"If the drug dealer learned to use his skills the right way, he could be a Fortune 500 leader.

We always need to honor and value children and what they know. Chameleon Children can turn toward the light or the darkness. We must assess each child within a personality style and ask ourselves, "Where is this child at this time?" says Koch.

The Diva Child

If a youth is denied attention, he or she may use standing-out behavior to get it. This is the Diva Child who loves the stage and the limelight. Anger and frustration are usually just below the surface for the Diva Child. When he does not get the attention wanted, he may exhibit sudden outbursts, including self-injurious and risk-taking behaviors. These behaviors can also be signs of more meaningful emotional problems such as trauma. When promiscuous behavior surfaces in the Diva Child, it may be more than just attention getting. It may signal sexual abuse. The Diva Child becomes attached to those deemed worthy of their affections or those who can supply what they need for survival. Sometimes outwardly confident, the Diva Child can be deceptive. These children must be taught appropriate strategies for meeting their needs. Negative or dangerous behaviors need to be replaced with healthy ones.

The Invisible Child

The Invisible Child avoids calling attention to self. These children are quiet bystanders and followers. They seldom give an opinion and defer to the majority. Others easily lead them, and they readily change their morals and ethics to suit a situation that offers comfort and security. Invisible Children may have serious issues with physical contact. They may come from abusive backgrounds. They do not easily show emotion, such as anger or hurt. While they may look content on the exterior, underneath they may feel dead. Cutting-behaviors may indicate a need to prove that they *do* have feelings. These youth are withdrawn from the world, often due to serious trauma.

"All of these children may turn to self-injurious behaviors to feel, not feel, communicate, or punish themselves," says Koch.

TRAUMA SURVIVORS AND THE TRICKSTER TALE

Many cultures have Trickster tales. Among the Native Americans we find Coyote and Raven, Africa has Anansi, and the Norse have Loki. A common element in the Trickster tale is the character's ability to teach humanity through folly. The Trickster places another character in a situation where either that other character or the Trickster must make a choice and experience the consequences. This usually leads to the demise of the one making the choice, yet a lesson is always learned. The Trickster has no problem remaining a casual observer, letting the other characters solve the problem on their own. If Tricksters are the ones experiencing the challenge, they either learn a lesson or remain untouched by that experience. This is often seen in an Anansi story where he continues to be foolish, goes on to the next story, and is foolish again. This may be a valuable lesson for at-risk youth. The Trickster allows us to have complete experiences and to continue to be who we are after that experience. In addition, the Trickster is often hurtful to a character, but not to the listener who sees the action played out from a safe distance.

> "In some ways, the Chameleon Child may be playing the role of the Trickster that is different from a story Trickster. Unlike the story Trickster, children who play with emotions do hurt others without a lesson being learned. When we work with co-dependent children, we have to ask them "What would you have to give up if you weren't saving the world?" This helps them understand how addictive that becomes. They may have to give up feeling important or feeling special to feel sane.
>
> Tricksters seldom have stillness in their lives. Stillness is hard for a Chameleon Child to learn. These children play the role of parent and take risks to save those they want to protect. For example, they may sacrifice themselves because they feel responsible to siblings or their mothers by stepping between them and an abuser. They do not always think through the consequences for this risk and place themselves in danger. Stillness, a moment of presence before action, would be of great value to them.

Stillness happens when a story is told. The listener enters a trance state without anyone asking them to go there. The act of listening in this state is self-soothing. However, if we tell trauma victims that they have to listen and be still, they lose control and may feel re-victimized.

The Trickster offers these children an opportunity to enter the story as an observer in the stillness of that moment and experience the folly of others. They are allowed to laugh at these mistakes. For the child who has Trickster qualities, we can find value in these skills. He might be manipulative, negative, or adaptive.

The goal is to tailor these skills so the Trickster can use them without having to be outwardly focused on using them against someone else."

Diana Koch

A true Trickster is a creative spirit and teacher. Unlike Coyote in the Roadrunner cartoons who always experiences the hurt he tries to inflict on the victim, a true Trickster teaches us through actions and mistakes.

"Trickster teaches, as does a storyteller, in such a way that listeners do not know they are being taught. Trickster puts listeners in places they do not expect to be and gives them challenges that allow them to make good or bad choices.

The difference between Trickster and the Chameleon Child, who is highly empathetic, is that the Trickster has distress tolerance that lets him sit back and see people go through the pain of growth. He can challenge and manipulate the others or sit back and let them wallow in it. This allows the others to move themselves through the story. Chameleon Children feel they have to move people through it by becoming caregivers who martyrs themselves. A Chameleon Child can do for others, but is unable to let others do for him. Receiving a gift is an art."

Diana Koch.

Katie was a child I worked with for a short period. In fact, I only saw her five or six times over two months. What I remember most about her was her need for attention and how she allowed her Trickster self to take over when she was desperate to get what she wanted. Katie had many acting-out behaviors. She was a Diva Child, bright and totally willing to do what pleased me. She loved compliments about how well she did and wanted others to applaud her strengths. Still, Katie could not accept a gift without giving one in return.

We had one of our sessions on Valentine's Day. I decided to give each child a Valentine gift. I gave Katie a little bear holding a heart. She took it, jumped to her feet, and said, "I'll be right back." Without any explanation or thanks, Katie ran off to her room. She returned moments later with an obviously well-loved stuffed pink rabbit. "Here," she said and handed it to me.

Katie was very generous because she parted with one of her own toys in exchange for mine. Yet, inwardly I suspect Katie could not accept my gift without making us "even" by giving me one in return. In this way, Katie never had to worry that I might "use" my gift against her later.

> "The best caregivers receive as well as give. We are not ready to help others if we cannot do this. We also need to resist the urge to step in and carry the child out of danger too fast.
>
> Trauma might be triggered even if people present safe gifts. The trauma survivor is reminded of the grooming process or when those who were supposed to take care of them abused, hurt, or left them. They always ask themselves 'What do they want from me?' 'What if I take it and later they want something?' Taking a gift is risking connection,"
>
> *Diana Koch.*

SEXUALITY AND THE AT-RISK TEEN

Decisions about sexuality are difficult for the "average" teenager and doubly so for youth at-risk. Working with teens requires understanding the complexity of relationships.

Many at-risk girls have had abusive experiences, leaving them confused at a vulnerable stage in life. Patterns that feel familiar, even when bad for them, may give them comfort. It is also at this time of the awkward teen years that youth experiment with their sexuality. They may take multiple partners or partners of the same sex, either because they are curious or because they find safety in it. It is also not unusual to find name-calling and sexual labeling used as a means of controlling and hurting others either out of cruelty, lack of understanding, or jealousy. These "buttons" are powerful and other teens know it. As caregivers, we should be careful not to second-guess the truth of a teen's sexuality before exploring the teen's background and getting to know him or her better.

Teens are still learning about their sexuality. Both at-risk girls and boys can be more vulnerable and susceptible to pressure for acceptance. They may be in serious need of security, protection, food, or shelter. Sex may or may not be part of these relationships, but it can be used as a bargaining chip to purchase what is needed. When the need is strong enough, even the toughest youth may succumb to behaviors outside their usual lifestyle.

Regardless of sexual orientation, youth in need of comfort and security will take what is offered without asking questions of themselves and others. This can pose a serious threat to the Chameleon Child who may choose a sexual partner to fit in or get help.

Some youth will experiment and some may discover their sexual identities. This can include everything from heterosexual, homosexual, bisexual, and transgender activity. Sexuality is a normal human experience and teens are biologically sexual beings, but for Chameleon girls, sex may be used for conformity and survival. While Chameleon boys sometimes use sexual favors, these boys are more likely to meet survival needs through illicit and violent means.

Our society's concept and understanding of sexuality is widening; nevertheless, teens who are already struggling with their feelings and confused by messages received through the media and their peers may need professional assistance.

Organizations exist in support of homosexual, bisexual, and transgender youth and their issues, though they are few and far between. These organizations are necessary for these teens to receive services important for their safety and health.

Supportive adults must acknowledge sexual conflict when working with at-risk youth. It is just one more piece of the puzzle and dance of these young people and we cannot afford to be surprised by their behaviors and what they say to us. Some of it will be real, and some will be sensational, designed to throw us off-balance. It is best to be aware and not appear shocked and appalled. These behaviors are partnership-testing mechanisms.

> "Traumatized children may engage in victim or perpetrator sexual behaviors. They may lack the skills to stop the behaviors. They have internalized the idea of the non-protective bystander, adults not intervening to help them. Others may have blamed them for the abuse or disqualified their feelings.
>
> Every girl who calls herself a lesbian is not necessarily a lesbian in the true sense of the word. Research shows that only about 10% of the population is at that end of the sexuality continuum, and it is a continuum. Chemical makeup forms sexuality. Most people who are truly gay often sense a difference in early life. Sexual behavior is different for each child. We see it manifested in the need to claim somebody, to be able to say, 'That person's with me. That person's mine.' Teens are going through a stage in their growth of being highly sexual and aroused. Their bodies are changing and we have to consider that. It is a vulnerable time."
>
> *Diana Koch*

FOLLOWING THE CROWD

A young person may become a follower to gain favors from others. The need for acceptance has a strong pull and peer pressure for at-risk youth who are dealing with so many complex issues can be harder to resist. As previously mentioned, these behaviors are survival techniques. Keeping an open mind allows us a better opportunity for changing these behaviors. If a youth has turned to an inappropriate behavior for survival, we need to help them find a replacement survival technique or somehow meet that youth's needs. Simply telling them they are wrong constitutes a judgment and does not serve their best interest or solve the problem. Most will continue the behavior if no alternative is presented. Stories offer models for behavior changes. "Sir Gawain and the Green Knight" and "The Boy Who Thought He Was a Man" are just two examples of such stories. (Full stories can be found in *Dancing at the Crossroads: Stories and Activities for At-Risk Youth Programming*)

> "The piece that is missing for many Chameleon Children is the true ability to empathize. However, this is not true for all of these youth. In fact, the Chameleon Child can master empathy to receive enormous benefits from the relationship. Yet, what does not get attention is the understanding that we do not have to give to receive. The "feel good" gifts they receive from their own actions of giving can be so reinforcing that it is the core of their co-dependency. It is an addictive way of living and thinking that is hard to give up. These youth get their sense of well-being from this control and sense of affecting change. They use all their energies focusing on what other people want and are highly sensitive to the response. They abandon or leave self behind.
>
> The problem arises when the person with whom a youth associates begins to get clear or sober. Suddenly that person does not want the youth to do all the giving, because they know it is toxic for both. This is when families may start to crumble. When someone is in recovery, the one who was healthy must now adapt to the relationship, and they

find this difficult and stressful. The recovering person now wants their friends, partners, and relatives not to sacrifice themselves. They do not want everything done for them. Therefore, children who have not learned to receive with pleasure are setting themselves up with a formula for chaos and crisis.

In a situation where the child has negotiated to suit the needs of others, the fact that the child sacrificed and betrayed self is more painful than the threat the other enacted upon them. Chameleon children are so conditioned to betray themselves that they do not always realize they are doing it. Their sensitivity to the needs and wants of the outside world parallels their lack of awareness of any inner life or value in their own thoughts and feelings. They do not know they have a problem, which makes later healing and therapy difficult. They believe they have been successful because their needs were met. "

Diana Koch

GANGS AND THE ADOLESCENT

Just as various behaviors serve a purpose for at-risk teens, youth gangs may supply their missing families. The following is an interview with ex-gang leader, Luis Acosta of Buffalo, New York.

At the time this book was written, Luis has turned his life around. He is the founder and CEO of Urban Community Corporation, a not-for-profit organization founded in 1999 and based in Buffalo, New York, that trains ex-convicts in the building trade. Luis is an entrepreneur who saw a need based on his own experience and created a solution. A one-time gang member and ex-convict, Luis found it difficult to start over after his release from prison. He saw the same thing happening to the young men and women in his community, so he took action. In an effort to thank his wife, parents, brother, and friends for their support of his efforts, Luis generously offered his personal insights on why teens join gangs and what we as adult community members can do to help them.

INTERVIEWER: Why are kids drawn to gangs?

LUIS: I've been given an opportunity. After going through the life I've gone through, I can help these young men and women and show them there is a better way.

I was a former gang member, starting at age twelve. I didn't know what I was getting into. Our neighborhood was a predominantly black neighborhood. I didn't know I had to walk through a territory. It belonged to a gang in Rochester called "the Crusaders."

The first time I walked through the neighborhood I was scared and I ran. One day when I came home, not crying you know, my mother seen [*sic*] worry in my face. I was teary-eyed. She told me not to cry anymore because I had to take care of myself out there. My mother couldn't fight all my battles.

I went back and I defended myself, only I didn't know the person I fought was the second in that age bracket, the Juniors.

The Crusaders had a huge group. I gained my respect throughout the Eastside and collaborated with the Hispanic gang in the area. We formulated a group. My associates and I changed the name of the former Hispanic gang and made it a lot bigger. There were almost two hundred sixty-five kids within six months, a lot more within a year. That took me to a place where I felt indestructible. Kids with the same situations gathered and gave our thoughts. We protected each other because we was [*sic*] considered as family. We have to protect each other out here.

INTERVIEWER: Would you say that's why most kids get involved with gangs?

LUIS: The reasons why they get involved with gangs, one is because of the family setting. They don't have family at home, so they look for family in the street. Then there are those who are peer-pressured to become gangs. Those are the individuals who are in mostly for protection or just want to be hanging out with the crew that is, you know, part of the fad of that month, or whatever the case might be. He will present himself sooner or later, because someone really involved in a gang can protect those who are not. It's really family. That's the first and most important reason kids get into the gang.

INTERVIEWER: So what do you think adults can do?

LUIS: I believe they should start seeing the truth. You see every generation had gangs. Every culture that came to America had gangs. If you look back, even in the times of George Washington, when the United States was Colonialist and people were just migrating here, there were gangs that defended their territories. You had the "Mad Hatters." You had the "Crazy Rabbits." You had various gangs for various ethnic groups in the 1800s. You had the Italians, Irish, Jewish, Polish, and Dutch, and the ones who were born in the United States that wanted to protect their neighborhoods. To be honest with you, the birthplace of gangs is really in New York City and the "five points." So the thing is, we look so hard to find why kids are into gangs when we just need to look at where gangs started and the process that made gangs what they have become. Gangs are Republicans and Democrats.

INTERVIEWER: What would you say to a mother, a father, or a family who had some idea that their kid was involved in a gang and worried that they were going to be shot in the street one day?

LUIS: Well, what I always say is that "a gang" is misunderstood. To me, gangs are the lost Generation X. To me, they are God's Anointed New Generation: G-A-N-G. They're God's kids. What we need to do is to start putting emphasis on wanting to relate with these kids. Hear what they say. We have told them what they need to do instead of listening to what they have to do. So, I think if any parent looks at the history of where gangs come from, they will understand why kids are in gangs today. You know the saying, "If you look at your past, you'll find your future.

The past is in the 1800s when people first migrated here. They were all gang members who protected, in fact many became police, fire chiefs, governors. The first mayor of New York, his name is Tinomy, built City Hall. He was one of the first Irish gang members in America. There is still the Irish mafia, the Italian mafia, Jewish mafia and so on. They are all descended from the first gangs that were here. They can trace their families back to the homeland.

INTERVIEWER: Should we be trying to get kids to not be involved with gangs?

LUIS: I believe the biggest problem that happened with gangs was letting people that have the resources enter and make gangs severe. They brought guns and drugs in our communities. Without the guns, the kids would just be a bunch of "punks" doing what they did in the 30s and 40s. The worst thing then was a bat or a knife. In today's society, weapons are very easy to access. You can't say the kids in the community are the ones developing the guns and the weapons. They're not. They're being brought to these kids to inflict harm on each other. There's a reason why all these weapons are here. If we deter the weapons, that would be a big stop to the violence, but as a parent, a person who is an adult, you have to listen to them. Then, work with their situation. Don't try to pull them out of the gang because the family is what they love the most. So, what you do is work with the gang. Don't work against them, because you need to gain their trust. If you don't, you'll never be able to open the door to take at least one kid out.

I have the opportunity and the pleasure of saving a lot of kids in my community, but nobody knows. Not the police, not the city, not the mayor. I don't get hero's awards. I wouldn't be considered the person who stopped a murder beef. In their minds, it's not applicable. Because I know how to relate with the kids and understand that the gang is their family, I work not only with the kid, but with his whole sect. I understand what are "his" problems. Why isn't he eating? Why does he only have a pack of cigarettes in the refrigerator? You have to look at those things. So, you have to work with his emotional needs, not give him what he needs, but help him achieve what he needs.

INTERVIEWER: What are you doing now?

LUIS: I developed a not-for-profit organization after my incarceration. I committed a crime by defending myself. I shot an FBI informant who tried to put me in the judicial system. He tried to obligate me to be part of the drug trade. I did five and a half years, but it taught me a lesson. It taught me that a lot of our young men and women are going through the same thing when they come home, they don't have nothing [*sic*] to look forward to, so they end up back in incarceration. And, I thank God he has given me a dream to help the young people in our communities, those with financial or educational problems. I developed a peer apprenticeship program in the building trade. It is compatible with ESL [English as a Second Language], college, and individuals who want to apply for their GED [Graduate Equivalent Diploma]. We want to be able to pay as they learn so they can provide for their families, at the same time educate themselves and move their dreams forward. They may want to enter college, open their own business, work for a company, or enroll in a union. We'd like to be able to help them purchase their own homes. We anchor our young men and women, even those individuals that were gang leaders who could bring thirty to forty people to the table. We want to show them they are leaders in every way. They can help deter individuals who are going through the very same experience.

I'm a product of what I'm preaching because I'm living it myself. That's why I speak about it. To pull a person out of a situation requires creating ways to help them become independent of what's keeping them in that same blighted community. By hatching a community and teaching them how to do it, they can become free of the community, but stay anchored in the community to save it.

I am the founder and CEO of the Urban Community Corporation. We hope to move beyond Buffalo into every major city in the United States. We deal with the community as a whole. To change a community you need to be able to put food on the table so they can think about the other things that are needed.

I've been working on this plan since 1999. We've even created software to help people build a portfolio instead of a resume to show a visual of their accomplishments through a website. They can learn in the classroom or at home. We will teach them to fix abandoned buildings as they are being trained on the site.

Thanks to my brother, my team, and my wonderful wife. My mother and father have been a tool of my growth. They showed me that morals and respect to everyone is the key of success. As a poor man speaking to you today, I am the richest man in the world because I'm making a change not only for myself, but for the community. This is from the bottom of my heart.

When dealing with youth involved in gangs or those who claim gang membership, we need to remain mindful of safety. Even though many youth think of gangs as family, gang activity can be very real and deadly. A "wannabe" youth has more to prove than an actual gang member and therefore can be more volatile. It is advisable not to challenge their supposed membership but to acknowledge their reason for wanting to be part of a gang. Colors, tattoos, symbols, hand signs, clothing, and speech may be signposts of gang activity. Many city police departments now have gang units, and adult caregivers who are concerned should contact their local police authority for assistance, because the danger to the youth and the adult may be very real.

The interview with Luis provides an inside view of street life and how our young people view what they are doing. Keeping an open mind and really listening is something we need to take with us when working with today's youth. We must learn to separate the behavior from the child and deal with those things we have power over— *our* actions and reactions. We can change their behavior only through *our* example and by presenting options to our children.

Chapter 2
Changing Behaviors

VIEWPOINT IS EVERYTHING WHEN TRYING TO UNDERSTAND TEENS. How they view their behaviors may be different than how we view them. It is a matter of who decides what is acceptable or unacceptable. Different ideas can easily lead to misunderstanding. Clarity of vision is the best way to move forward toward a solution. We need to ask our youth how *they* feel and what *they* think about the things that directly relate to their lives. Again, we are looking for a negotiable situation. Problem solving can come by force or through open-mindedness. We will only achieve lasting peace through the latter, because force leads to resentment. Our goal is to find a replacement behavior and convince the young person that it is better for them. We should consider what we know about our expectations and realize that we can offer controlled choices. This means giving several acceptable solutions from which to choose and allowing the youth to choose within those safe options. By doing so, we reverse viewpoints on behaviors and prove them as safe or unsafe, rather than right or wrong, which is a matter of opinion.

> Before we can expect young people to risk learning new ways of coping, we need to honor the function and validness of their behaviors. Then we hope they will risk exploring our suggestions.
>
> It takes a lifetime to learn to be intuitive and draw on the lessons our mentors have taught us, instead of relying on the crowd. As caregivers we hope our young people will listen to what we have to teach them and use these lessons later in life. The tragedy is that many of today's at-risk youth do not

have strongly woven guidelines to follow. Our purpose as adult caregivers is to keep our children safe and teach them to cope and survive on their own.

Individuals and families do not experience trauma in a vacuum. By treating the whole, perhaps the family will come together to learn and hear each other's stories. Separation comes from the inability to do this. The issues consume them. Once they collectively create a family story about what has happened to them, they come together.

Diana Koch

The Pickle Jar

We do not always realize the value of the help we give. As with a pickle jar that we cannot open, if we pass it along a line of people, someone will eventually loosen the lid. In truth, everybody loosened it a little bit. We may not be there when it finally opens because therapy and healing take time. Each of us plants a seed."

On the other hand, trying to heal is not necessarily about knowing that we affected a change. We need to honor our client's choices and what they do with what we give them. Sometimes the best we can do for a trauma survivor is give them that choice. Even if they decide not to take, we were somebody who did not force it on them.

Diana Koch

A STORY OF NASTAI

This is a Saami story from Lapland titled "A Mother's Yarn," it may be found in a collection of stories of women heroes (Riordan, 1962. *The Woman in the Moon and Other Tales of Forgotten Heriones*). In this story, the main character survives by using the skills her mother taught her.

A Mother's Yarn

Nastai lived in the farthest reaches of Lapland with her mother and father. Her mother was a strong and wise woman. In fact, it was Nastai's mother who hunted and fished. She cooked and made everything the family needed for survival. Nastai's father was content to sit and watch his wife and daughter at their work. They were happy and well off. The family had feather mattresses, a fine herd of reindeer, and furs to keep them warm.

Then there came a time of great suffering. An illness spread across the land and came to Nastai's home. Her mother and father both fell ill and while the old man recovered, his wife did not.

"Remember everything I have taught you," said Nastai's dying mother. "Take care of the old man and make sure he is well."

Nastai promised and when her mother died she did just that. Nastai cared for her father until he regained his health. She herded the reindeer, fished, hunted, cooked, and cleaned.

News traveled fast of the wise woman's death, and it came to the broken-down hut of a beggar-woman and her daughter. Their reindeer herd was gone and all that was left was an aged buck. They had no furs and the roof of their house leaked. The woman and her daughter had no food, but that was no problem since they simply begged their neighbors for what they needed to eat. All was provided for them. When the beggar-woman heard that the old wise woman was dead, she decided to visit the old man.

She and her daughter hitched the old buck to their sleigh and off they went. The old beggar was pleased to see the well-tended herd grazing lazily around the old man's house. She was pleased to see the strong fat dogs that guarded the herd. Best of all was the old man who sat comfortably in his furs beside the house. His daughter Nastai was nowhere to be seen.

"Are you the old widower?" asked the beggar.

"I am," replied the man.

"Then I am telling you now that I am the new woman of this house."

The old beggar and her daughter moved right in. When Nastai returned home, she was surprised to find a strange woman and a young girl in her father's house. Her father sat at the table banging a spoon against an empty pot with drool running down his chin. He was quite drunk and an empty wine skin lay upon the table.

"Do we have guests, Father?" asked Nastai.

"I am no guest!" replied the beggar-woman. "I am the woman of this house. Is that not so old man?"

Nastai's father could only nod his head as he fell forward on the table.

Nastai brought food for the old woman and her daughter. She spread fresh straw on the floor and covered the feather mattress with furs. The old woman and her daughter ate then crawled into bed to sleep.

After many days, the old woman began to think of ways to get rid of Nastai. One day she said "Old man, load up all your most valuable possessions. We will go to my land where the hunting will be better. Your daughter will stay here in her mother's house."

She helped the old man put all his pots, furs, hunting spears, his bow and arrows, and feather mattresses on her sleigh. They herded the reindeer before them. Nastai was left alone with no furs to keep her warm and no food to stave her hunger. The girl cried.

As she sat there alone weeping, she heard a voice. "Nastai, look around you."

Nastai did look around her, but all she saw was a scrap of twisted yarn upon the floor. Then Nastai recalled how her mother would always throw one piece of the yarn she spun upon the floor. She picked it up and heard the voice again.

"Remember what I have taught you."

Recalling how her mother hunted, Nastai took the yarn and made a lasso of it. She took it into the forest and placed it upon the ground. She waited patiently and at last caught one lame bird. Nastai took it home and stripped the sinew from its legs. She used this to make another lasso. The new one caught two larger birds that she plucked and used for meat. But, Nastai had no cook fire or pot.

Again she heard the voice "Nastai, remember what I taught you."

The girl returned to the forest and cut a birch branch. She removed its long strips of bark and wove a bowl. She coated the bowl with clay and dried it in the sun. Now Nastai had a pot to cook her meat. After gathering kindling of moss and pinecones, she found flint and stone to make a spark. The hungry girl cooked and ate, then set her traps again.

After many days of trapping birds, Nastai had a large pile of feathers. She slept on the pile, but the feathers tickled her nose and made her sneeze, so Nastai made a spindle and distaff of wood. The girl used down and veins to spin a cover to fill with feathers.

Now Nastai had plenty to eat and was warm and dry. But, the girl grew lonely.

"Nastai, remember what I taught you."

She returned to the forest and pulled up a small pine. Nastai used its roots to make a strong lasso. She waited for a reindeer herd. When a little fawn passed by, Nastai caught it in the lasso. She led the little deer home and after a while it followed her just as if she were its mother.

Now winter was upon her and Nastai had no food left, no hat, no coat, and no boots to wear.

"Remember what I taught you," the voice said again.

Nastai went to the lake. She used a willow tree to make a bow and arrows. The girl now hunted in the falling snow. First she took a squirrel and then a fox. Before too long, Nastai had enough furs to make warm winter clothing. One day, when she returned from hunting, Nastai found the fawn's mother had come following the scent of her young. One by one, more deer appeared and Nastai had a small healthy herd of reindeer.

As the girl sat in the warmth of her house, she thought of the coming spring and worried that her herd would leave when the snows melted.

"Remember what I taught you."

Nastai spent the next day searching the forest for a wolf den. She found one with a mother and four cubs. Nastai took the cubs when their mother was away and raised them to guard her herd. Soon, they were very skilled. Nastai had everything she needed and was successful.

A year had passed and the old beggar-woman and her daughter had squandered everything. They had traded away the old man's wealth, eaten all their food, and had not repaired their house. Only the old buck remained.

"Hah," spat the old woman. "We will return to Saami land where you can fish and hunt again."

She offered no assistance or sympathy to either the old man or her own daughter. Her only solution was to take what was left at the old man's house. And she thought, "That girl will be dead by now anyway."

As the three neared Nastai's house, they saw wood smoke rising through the chimney. They saw a healthy herd of reindeer grazing, well-fed dogs, and a well-kept hut. Nastai herself sat beside the house bundled in furs. She saw them coming.

"Welcome Father. You must be hungry and tired," she said. "Come inside and eat hot broth and rest in my featherbed."

It was as if a spell were broken. When the old man looked around him and saw his daughter's face, he at last opened his mouth and screamed, "You evil woman! Be gone and take your daughter with you!"

Before the old beggar could reply, the old man slapped the buck and the woman's sleigh took off, dragging the beggar back to her own lands.

Nastai's father never again strayed from his daughter's home for the rest of his days.

The value in this story is not its ending. The story's power resides in the girl's struggle to maintain the house and keep it. This is an important concept for at-risk teens. So often, they are left with nothing. They lose all hope for bettering themselves and develop a defeatist attitude. Nastai's success is their success.

The voice that keeps reminding Nastai, "Remember what I have taught you," is the other powerful element of this story. As in the story of Vassalisa (page 37 in *Dancing at the Crossroads: Stories and Activities for At-Risk Youth Programs*), Nastai's mother has left her daughter a legacy. She taught her the basics of survival, which is what happens in a healthy parent-child relationship. This voice is not the actual voice of her mother, but Nastai's deep psyche giving rise to the knowledge she needs. At times these lessons are not in place before a child becomes a young adult. If a child has been given the knowledge needed, there is little room for doubt and failure.

We cannot erase negative imprints in children who come from abuse, neglect, and abandonment. We can lessen the impact these tragedies have on them, but it takes time. There is no quick fix. It takes years of patience, understanding, love, teaching, compassion, trust, respect, and hard work. There will be many instances when we think we have found a level of success only to experience a regression into old habits and negative behavior. There is no substitute for persistence when adults enter the crossroads and dance with at-risk teens. Frustration and sadness will be close companions on the journey.

THE "I DON'T KNOW" SYNDROME

When asking a youth for their opinions, ideas, thoughts, or feelings on any given issue, we need to remain open-minded. Their answers may not be the ones we want to hear and may not seem outwardly sensible. The best policy is to ask open-ended questions that require descriptive answers and go beyond singular yes or no replies. We must be prepared to accept their responses and it may be necessary to look below the surface to discover the truth.

A Chameleon Child may mask his or her truths to remain anonymous by saying, "I don't know." This answer may seem unprofitable, yet looking deeper we can find something of value. There are many subtle definitions for "I don't know." Possibly, the youth truly lacks knowledge and familiarity with the topic, some may lack the vocabulary with which to express themselves or may be confused by the question and their feelings. Many people do not verbally express themselves well. One way to avoid this problem is through artwork. Using it as an alternative form of expression requires different brain functions and offers the Chameleon Child an opportunity for protection from emotional exposure. Artwork has other functions too. As a tool for telling a story, it eliminates stage fright. When young people talk about how they created their work of art, they often tell the story without knowing that they have done so.

Young people also respond with "I don't know" when they have low self-esteem, no personal preference, or are indifferent. Teens lacking self-esteem are afraid to sound foolish by giving the wrong answer. They may also be telling us they have no interest in the issue and have not given it any thought. Perhaps they have decided it is not important to them. On the other hand, a youth could be using this reply as a form of rebellion. "I don't know," might actually mean, "You're crazy if you think I am going to tell you anything."

As questioners, we must be sincere. At-risk teens have heard the rhetoric so many times that it has become meaningless for them. They wonder if we really care when we ask, "How do you feel about that?" How young people react to our questioning will depend on their experiences. Each situation should be considered unique and approached freshly, without judgment and expectation. Again, the quest is for meaning.

"I don't know," may be an avoidance that can happen for any number of reasons. The teen might feel uncomfortable talking about the issue. It might be too difficult to face. Perhaps they feel guilty about something. To hide something they have done, teens may lie about their feelings, again from guilt. "I don't know" is the easiest reply they can give. This easy statement is safe and comfortable. We must patiently persist and wisely read between the lines.

"Often, children and youth who have grown up in addictive family systems learned that what they knew or felt depended on what someone else knew or felt. For example, whatever the alcoholic father was feeling determined the state of the family in that moment," says Koch.

FEELING GUILTY

Guilty feelings cause conflict both within an individual and in a relationship, especially when coupled with low self-esteem. Teens struggle to figure out how they feel, how they should cope with those feelings, and how to repair whatever went wrong. If self-injurious and suicidal behaviors are *not* present, this introspection can be helpful. Thoughtful consideration before action is always better than reaction to raw emotion. This is true for caregiver and youth alike, and we must keep the lines of communication open, allowing teens to sort through the problem, reminding them we are here when they are ready.

We should not highlight the problem, often seen as nagging by teens who are already trying to understand their feelings and behaviors. Waving the mistakes in their faces only causes an explosion of emotion, pushing them farther from us. At these times of intense emotion, it is more beneficial to let them know we understand their conflicts and are there if they need to talk. Our willingness to step back and listen is actually less threatening than forcing our will on them.

"For some youth, guilt is a feeling that helps them avoid the reality of the experience of having control taken away from them," says Koch.

Part II

Learning to Dance and Our Relationship with At-Risk Youth

Chapter 3
Negotiating Separation

Dancing is a continuous, pattern-forming motion. Think of the ice at an ice skating exhibition. When the skaters leave the ice, their path patterns remain. Follow the trail and we may find the starting point, or we may discover the pattern is so interwoven we cannot tell beginning from end. We may become lost in the design. That is the dance we do with ourselves and with our youth. Sometimes the objective is clear and sometimes it is not. Life patterns can be more complex for at-risk teens, especially victims of trauma.

"Triggers, or reminders of trauma, can rise without displaying their patterns or showing the road back to the original event. Youth may react to current stressors without being able to connect the dots to the trigger and its origin. This can bring up continued feelings of confusion, fear, and defectiveness," says Koch.

In this relationship dance, the adult, inner child, and teen may find themselves constantly moving toward and then away from each other. How we negotiate forward movement determines how long we stay together. If done incorrectly, we may move apart forever, and never dance in the same place again. The story of "The Tiger's Whisker" is an excellent example of a technique for successful negotiation.

The Tiger's Whisker

Once there was a man and a woman who were very much in love, but something happened to the man that made him angry and cruel to his wife. When she placed his supper in front of him, he pushed it away.

"Don't give me that. You can't cook," he criticized.

She tried to please him, but he only forced her away and said she couldn't do anything right. The woman was angry and sad. She knew this was not the husband she married and wanted to find him again, so she went to visit the wise man of her village. Everyone said that this man could cure any illness and had many potions for such troubles.

"I can help bring your husband back to you," the wise man said. "But, I will need the whisker of a tiger."

"The whisker of a tiger?" asked the woman. "How can I get such a thing?"

"I will need it if you want your husband back."

And so the woman returned home, certain she would never see her husband again and very saddened by the thought. Yet, she didn't give up. She thought throughout the night and finally a plan came to her.

There was a tiger living in a cave outside the village. The next morning, the woman went to the butcher and bought a juicy slab of fresh meat. This she carried it to the tiger's cave. She stood several yards away and placed the meat on the ground. She moved back and hid.

The tiger smelled meat and came from the cave. Though the woman was hidden from sight, the tiger seemed to stare at her. His massive body rippled with muscles as he drew close to the meat. He sniffed the woman's scent on the air then dragged the meat into the cave.

The next day and the next, the woman did the same until one day she was able to drop the meat at the mouth of the cave. She drew away, but not as far as before. The tiger came and ate the meat. Finally, after many days, the woman stood and placed the meat at her feet. The tiger eyed her, but he did not molest her. Instead he sat and ate at her feet. Then there came a day when the woman fed the beast right from her hand. While she trembled with fear, she did not run, nor did the tiger do her harm. On the next day, after the tiger had eaten from her hand, he placed his head in her lap and fell asleep. When she was certain he would not wake, she gently moved his head aside to the ground, quickly plucked a whisker from the tiger's muzzle, and ran as fast as she could to the wise man's hut.

"I have it! I have it!" she shouted excitedly as she waved the whisker in the air.

The wise man looked up from his work. He squinted his eyes in disbelief. "Amazing," was all he said as he reached for the whisker. "You did get it."

Then just as quickly as she had plucked the whisker, the wise man tossed it into the fire and burned it.

"Are you insane?" the woman cried. "Do you know what I had to do to get that? Now how will you make my potion?"

"Woman," said the wise man. "You have no need for potions. How did you get the whisker, I wonder?"

"I worked each day at bringing the tiger closer to me so that I could get it. When he was relaxed and tame, I took it."

"Then you do not need a potion. You already know how to win your husband back again."

The woman smiled and left the wise man's hut. She returned home, and in time she and her husband returned to their happy life together.

The Homecoming of an At-Risk Youth

At-risk teens need to learn anger management skills. This story models for them how to get close to those they care about. It shows them how others perceive their anger. It teaches the value of trust and patience for negotiation. The first act in negotiation is to gain trust and set up a win-win environment. Caregivers working with angry or sullen youth need these skills as well. This is especially true when a youth returns home after an extended absence. Too many adults forget that these children coming home are more like strangers than family.

The relationship between parents and their teens who have returned home can break down in the absence of advance planning. Expectations and changes in point-of-view cannot be one-sided. If the relationship is to work, both parties must make compromises or else agree to accept all terms unconditionally. Empathy, the ability to understand how others feel, must be learned and practiced. The ability to accept the thoughts and feelings of others should not be confused with total agreement, nor can we give youth complete freedom to do as they please. They still need guidance, but negotiation requires balance.

"When a child leaves home in the midst of chaos and then returns, both child and adult have had an experience. Walls were built to contain the hurt from the prior chaos and subsequent pain of being disconnected. They were not able to protect or be protected by another. It will take time to risk moving toward each other again," says Koch.

The basic truths in the story of "The Tiger's Whisker" can also relate to dismantling the tower, the invisible shield around an emotionally injured individual. It takes time, patience, and trust. Expecting a damaged relationship to fully heal in a short time is unrealistic. In fact, it may never be the same again. When returning to the family, a young person may always be a visitor. In other words, they may always maintain their independence and never again fully prescribe to family ideologies. When a wayward youth returns home, it is vital for the parents and the youth to know the ground rules. Will you have an open door policy? Will there be restriction on movement and activities? Without these ground rules in place, understood and accepted by both parties, the reunion will not succeed.

As in our story mending a relationship is a matter of patience and trust. While it may sound simplistic, the principle is sound. If they have heard it before, teens request this story because it resonates with them and is filled with hope. They love the idea that they can tame the tigers in their lives, and for us as caregivers, we can find hope in our steadfastness toward these children.

The grand design in the parent/child relationship is for some separation to occur until the lines become so blurred it is hard to tell adult from child. Finally, the new adult-child will leave the nest. In the best of situations, parents continue in their role as parents, and children look to them for advice throughout their adult lives. The relationship becomes more symbiotic.

Eventually as we age, this role reverses and the child cares for the parent. That is the dance's finale; the partners switch roles and the student becomes the teacher.

This is not to say that relationships between partners will always follow a direct line. We cannot know who will have the lead role; this is decided early in a child's life. Yet, if this life-dance is to be completed successfully, the roles must eventually change. Children become adults who can care for themselves. Although not always able, these new adults should feel willing to care for their caregivers.

Unfortunately for many at-risk youth, their caregiving roles come way too early in life. Too often, children are expected to take care of themselves and their families when still very young. There are far too many parents being parented by their children. This is a responsibility children should not have until they are physically, emotionally, and mentally prepared to become adults.

Any break in the natural maturation pattern causes chaos later in life. When this happens and we refuse to let the dance have its natural pattern, we can cause conflict within the relationship. Separation may become permanent rather than occasional. Maturing into adulthood inevitably results in separation and is natural.

Imagine a string that holds the child to the parent. Some people call this the apron string or the umbilical cord. The parent can decide how much to let out and when to pull back. In doing so, the child learns the steps to the dance and the rhythms that make it work. They learn the difference between right and wrong and what is considered appropriate. Danger zones and taboos are clarified.

Balance is needed between what is safe and what is too rigid. If the parent holds too tightly and the child becomes a teen who struggles against the force of that string, it may snap, and when it does the teen is jettisoned out of control. Letting out a little at a time until the teen learns the rules is safer. It allows them to cope with the obstacles that come their way. On the other hand, if the parent allows the line to go too slack, the teen will grow without guidelines or boundaries. Observe couples on a dance floor. Some look stiff and we want them to loosen up a little. Others dance with such wild abandon it is almost embarrassing to watch them. Then there are those beautiful couples we enjoy watching because their dance is symbiotic. They match each other's movements and work together.

RULES

Teens will accept learning coping skills but may reject being forced to follow a set of rules. Although the meaning is about the same, it is a matter of effective word-crafting to eliminate conflict. We live in a world of partnerships not absolutes. While teens still need parenting, we must present ideas in ways they will find acceptable. Being a youth's friend is not the role we need to assume. They have plenty of friends. Instead, they require our guidance. We can offer our help without being forceful. We have a greater chance for success when we form partnerships where both parties establish how much or how little they are willing to accept and give.

Sylvia Nadler, retired director at Compass House Runaway Shelter and Resource Center offers two very important pieces of advice for dealing with at-risk youth:

1. A set of rules may be futile.
2. Leave the "buts" out of it.

   "I love you, *but* you have to . . . "

   "I care, *but* . . . "

   "I want him to come home, *but* . . . "

"But" is an excuse to fail. Every time we feel a "but" coming on, we should consider why we are objecting. When we say "but" we are not fully committed to what we are saying and have not fully embraced our convictions and our teens know it. We must be more honest with ourselves, say what we mean, and live up to what we say. Truth moves us toward mutual respect in any relationship, especially with teens. If we have to say, "You can come home, *but* you need to live by my rules," we are not really ready to give unconditionally.

Diana Koch relates the following story of a mother who was obsessed with the idea that her daughter must process the trauma to come home. She took her to many therapists, but anytime it came to the processing part, the girl found a way to act out.

The parent said "I can't take it anymore."

This was because she could not change it, fix it, or make it feel better. These were her expectations and it was painful for the parent and the child. It was as if the mother was saying to her daughter, "If you can just get past this our family will be okay."

All the responsibility was placed on the child. The child resented it because they were asking her to do work that was not hers to do.

Storyteller Marlaina Kreinin from Michigan says "We encumber ourselves with so many things that don't belong to us." We also encumber others.

Boundaries and Restrictions

We must have boundaries and restrictions. In fact, our young people want them.

To satisfy our adult responsibility toward our young people, and to give both parties what they need, we must be armed with all the facts. Knowledge is power. Not only must we be open with our true feelings, our youth must come to the table with their feelings too. We need realistic expectations for a successful reunion and should be prepared for setbacks.

Deception, trickery, and hidden agendas do not belong in a loving relationship. We must also remember that there are two sides to any dispute.

The following conversation was with a seventeen-year-old runaway girl who wishes to remain anonymous.

> "My mother doesn't let me do anything as a seventeen-year-old. She never lets me make my own decisions. She wants everything to be her way. She is overprotective. I wish she would meet a man. If I had a teenage child, I would give it freedom but with boundaries.
>
> 1. They can't come home in the morning.
> 2. If they want to go to a party, I will let them. But, they have to come home no later than midnight.
> 3. I will talk to them, even about drugs or sex."

This girl felt hemmed in and without control over her own destiny. She seemed to have a very good handle on what she wanted and how her mother might work with her to achieve it. Unfortunately, her mother did not listen and the girl never shared these feelings. She also never returned home.

Unconditional Love

Bleeding Heart

Lorna MacDonald Czarnota

Once there was an old mother who had three grown sons.

One day, her daughter-in-law, wife to the middle son and very much with child, sought her advice.

"Old Mother, I wonder what is a mother's love? A never-ending love?"

The young woman eased herself into a chair.

The old woman thought for a moment. "I still remember the day my oldest son was born. He had a handful of dark hair that stood straight up on the top of his head and I thought – he will be a thinker. My middle son, your husband, was not so gentle. He was a warrior. He kicked me from within, and when he was born, he kicked from without. He was a difficult child. But my youngest son, his head was made of stone. Where it took his brothers but a short time to learn their lessons, it took him years. If he was told that something was not good for him, he still had to try it on for himself, wear his own mistakes. He was stubborn, but I loved him just the same."

"That is what I mean, Old Mother. How can a mother love a child who is unworthy?"

The old woman motioned toward a flower in a vase on the table. "Daughter-in-law, do you know this flower?"

"Yes. It is the bleeding heart."

"A mother's love is like a bleeding heart. If her child skins his knee, her heart bleeds for him. If he does something wrong, her heart bleeds. If he does harm to himself or others, a mother's heart bleeds for her son."

"I do not understand," said the younger woman. "How can a mother love even then?"

"Look closely at the flower, Daughter-in-law. What do you see?"

The young woman leaned forward. "Where each petal is split a new white blossom emerges."

"And what else do you see?"

"Ah." sighed the young woman. "A seed. I see a seed."

"That is the seed of hope, and the secret of a mother's love. A mother must have hope for her children even if her heart is broken. That is a never-ending love."

The young woman smiled. "Now, I understand. Give me your hand, Old Mother."

And she placed the old woman's wrinkled hand on her belly. The child kicked.

"Ah," smiled the old woman. "It begins."

This story examines unconditional love. It asks whether we can continue loving those people who keep on hurting us. The impact of this story resides in the metaphor of the bleeding heart flower as a mother's heart. If you examine the flowers of the bleeding heart plant, you will find them layered, just as a relationship is layered. When they split open, you can see the seed inside. The seed is small, but it is the plant's life force.

This is a significant metaphor for unconditional love and a model for teaching our youth. Following the old mother's lead, we can give them room to answer the questions on their own, then accept their answers, even if they do not match our ideals completely. As questioners, if we feel they are heading in an unsafe direction with their replies, we can offer alternative solutions without saying theirs are wrong.

When discussing love, we must make a distinction between it and passion. Many young people have expectations for their relationships with us that fall far outside what is reasonable. Our love for them is not based on passion. Passion is emotionally based, whereas real love is more biological. We will not abandon them during emotional highs and lows, as sometimes happens in young love affairs.

Passion is not steadfast, it ebbs and flows. Teens need to know that the bonds between parent and child are stronger than that. Although those bonds will be tested often, our teens want to know that they will not break.

The news is full of stories about children who have committed horrific crimes, yet their parents still stand by them. We are bound to ask how this is possible. Unconditional love makes it possible. It remains strong even when emotions unravel because it is not formed around passion. We can accept and love another person while we condemn their behaviors or actions. We can separate the action from the person. We can find and give love without strings attached. We can love someone without liking him or her. This is the kind of love that keeps teens safe when their world comes crashing down around them. Unconditional love becomes the doorway for them to return to family. The family is their lifeline.

Teens may assume that their friends or partner will give them "true" love because they are accepted without judgment. When the going gets tough, these flimsy relationships crumble but that is better than nothing for some teens. Even family ties have no guarantees. Yet, if the family has built strong bonds in the early years of a child's development, chances are better that the teen will call on family in times of need.

Families must accept that they cannot control the time when a young person will be ready to return home. They must either remain constant and patient or give up the effort. Anything between leaves everyone underserved and frustrated.

When immediate family is not the lifeline of choice, teens will get help elsewhere. Rather than go to family for help, they have been known to live in their cars, sleep in burned out buildings, or worse. They are willing to tell their friends things they would never share with family. This may be because teens do not want to admit failure, and sometimes because they feel guilty. However, it is most likely because teens do not want to be ridiculed. This is introspective guilt. When feeling guilty, we only feel worse if ridicule is heaped on top of it. The guilt becomes unbearable. It is an art to listen without judgment and give love and advice unconditionally. I wrote the following poem for a friend.

Advice is a Gift We Give

A friend asked and I gave, she needed and I gave
It was a gift. I expected nothing in return.
I wanted only to know that it meant something.
A thank-you would be nice, a smile,
Yet I received nothing and
she did not use what I gave her.
I wanted to take it back. I could not.

I thought I would never give a gift again.
Was that fair to her? To me?
What did it matter if it went unused?
I didn't feel good when I didn't give,
So I gave again, again, again.
She saved them up, and one day
My gift saved her. That was good.

We can never really know how effective our love can be and we will only be effective if we try. Giving and receiving have nothing to do with each other but both are difficult skills to master; both leave us exposed.

Vulnerability and Conflict Resolution

The teen-dance is a sloughing of the child-skin, making the teen a bundle of raw energy, sensitive to any form of touch whether physical, emotional, or spiritual. Being careful how we approach them is important. Teens are vulnerable to strong suggestions from their peers, to our compliments or complaints, and to their own successes and failures, with failure being the harder of these to accept.

Conflict results when teachers, parents, or community leaders point out a teen's faults. They do not accept criticism well and we do not need to be as critical as we imagine we do. In most cases, teens know when they make a mistake. However, there are times when they may not know the difference between right and wrong. If that is the case, the situation must be handled differently. Our goal should be to make sure children have the concepts of right and wrong by the time they reach adolescence. When they do, our caregiving time can be spent teaching strategies and problem solving skills. If children do not know right from wrong, we must backtrack to teach the basics. Regardless, each youth requires special and individualized attention from us.

When interacting with someone, especially a teen who has made a mistake, consider the following to avoid conflict.

1. Acknowledge their intelligence and strengths and find ways to use those to *their* benefit.
2. If teens understand right from wrong, do they know what must be done to resolve the situation? Do they know how to begin? A lot of frustration can be eliminated if we realize that teens often lash out in frustration over lack of knowledge.
3. The young person may need us to open a door and offer guidance.
4. Assess each situation individually to find out exactly what the young person knows and what he or she is seeking.
5. We may find that their knowledge and their desires do not match. Our job is to help them find a match and execute a plan *without* our judgment of them.

Imagine, we have just entered a room and the doors have all slammed behind us. We feel helpless and trapped. Would we prefer someone to tell us how foolish it was not to prop the door open or would we prefer him or her to open a door? Do we want them to criticize what we did or give us a clue about how to fix it? Would we like to know which exit will lead us where we want to go or how "stupid" we were in the first place?

Sometimes we do not give our teens what they need. Instead, we waste our energy telling them what they already know. To avoid this we can ask ourselves a series of questions about our own actions, not about the youth. What is our goal?

1. Do we want to make sure our teens know they made a mistake?
2. Should we help them find a solution?
3. Do we need to teach them a method for discovering an answer?
4. Should we simply give them the solution?
5. How can we best help them cope?

In instances where the problem is dangerous or immediate, our choice of answers to these questions may be different. In a dangerous situation, we may need to find an immediate solution, always putting safety first.

Our actions toward a teen who is raw and vulnerable will either bring him to us or force him away, as in "The Tiger's Whisker." As we answer the questions above, we must always do what is best for the youth, not us.

This does not mean adults need to suffer endlessly. These battles can be emotionally draining, taking a toll on our well-being and our entire family. While we search for help for our youth, we need to take care of our own health.

WHEN IS ENOUGH, ENOUGH? TAKING CARE OF OURSELVES

A woman struggled to release herself from a harmful relationship between herself and her teen daughter. The struggle was extremely emotional, affecting her health and her family life. She made herself sick over it. This can easily happen to anyone.

Love is the most difficult human emotion to define and understand. We spend our entire lives trying to figure it out.

It is easy to think of unconditional love as selflessness or martyrdom, but it is not and we must find balance when we care for others. We cannot help another person if we are ill. In this precarious dance with at-risk teens, we must always preserve a sense of self. This is true in any relationship.

Relationships Built on Truth

The following story of the Black Prince, an Egyptian folktale popular among teens, tells of a poor young man who falls hopelessly in love with a beautiful princess. He runs away from home when he realizes the impossibility of this relationship. The boy finds a hermit who can change him into what he believes the princess would like so that he might win her heart, but he is warned that once this is done he cannot return to his former self. The irony of the story is that it was that poor simple boy the princess loved, not the powerful man he became, and so the story ends with the Black Prince walking off into the desert never to be seen again.

Teens do not applaud the story because it is sad and serious, but they do remember it. This is a powerful story that addresses the importance of being true to self. Relationships that are built on anything other than the truth are bound for failure. Retaining who we are is not selfish. In fact, we must sometimes give up a relationship when we are at risk of losing that sense of self.

The Black Prince

An Egyptian Folktale as told by Laura Simms*

In Ancient Egypt, there was a boy who was ugly, stupid, and lazy. The only thing he cared about was a wooden flute that he had carved. He would wander, play the flute, fall asleep. Even his mother said, "My son will come to nothing." She often said, "I expect that one day he'll fall asleep at the edge of the river and drown."

One day, while the boy was walking through the city, he came upon a white stone wall that he had never seen before. Beautiful green trees grew up behind the wall and, curious, he climbed to look at the garden. It was an extraordinary garden. But what truly caught his eye was a young woman, serene, beside a pool of water. The boy felt such longing that he wanted to play the flute. But the wind seemed to blow in the opposite direction.

He put the flute to his lips and he began to play softly everything he felt. When she didn't turn around, he was certain that she couldn't hear and he began to play everything he felt. He played all afternoon. And before the sun went down, she stood up and walked away, vanishing among the trees.

That night, he couldn't sleep. He couldn't stop thinking about the girl in the garden. And the next day he returned to the wall and waited. In the

*re-printed with permission of Laura Simms. This story can be found in *found in Ready-to-Tell Tales* by Holt and Mooney also in *Making Peace*, audio recording by Laura Simms on Earwig Recordings, Chicago

afternoon she returned. And once again, he played everything he felt. He returned to the garden every day.

He was falling in love. You know how it is the first time you fall in love. And each day he played the flute, played everything he felt. He fantasized that one day he would leap down into the garden, play music for her alone, and she would love him the way he loved her. He would ask her to marry him and she would go with him out of the garden to his mother's hut beside the river.

One evening, when he was returning home, he sat down by the well in the middle of the village to listen to the old women gossip. They were talking about a garden and he realized they were describing the very garden that he looked at every day. And the more he listened, the more he realized that the girl that he loved was none other than the pharaoh's daughter, the princess Thudmos.

He knew that a princess could not love a boy who was poor and ugly and lazy and stupid. He wandered through the city streets all night, broken-hearted. He couldn't go home.

Before dawn, he left the city gates, went out through the market, and there was a caravan of merchants. And the men bade him sit down with them and have some tea, and he did. And they told the kinds of stories that merchants tell, about magic. And he listened, all ears, as they described a magician named Habee: "He can do anything." And finally, the boy asked, "Can he change a man's soul?"

"Oh, God willing, if he's alive, he can change a man's soul. He performs miracles!"

"Where would I find him?"

And they pointed to the desert and told him to walk three days and three nights without stopping.

With nothing but the clothes on his back and his flute, the boy walked through the sand. He walked for three days and three nights without stopping. And he came to an oasis. There was a tree with a donkey tied to it and an old hut. The door opened, and an old man came out—bald, eyes wide, toothless.

"Are you Habee, the magician?"

"That is my name."

"I have heard that..."

"Boy, everybody hears about me. Everyone has a story. Rest. Refresh yourself. And then tell me your tale and what you would like."

The boy washed; he couldn't rest. And after drinking tea he waited until the magician sat down beside him. He explained who he was and how he had fallen in love with the pharaoh's daughter, and how she could never love him. And then he said to Habee, "Can you make me strong, powerful, charismatic, unrelenting, cruel–a soldier, a prince, a warrior?"

"Ha, ha, that I can do. But once I change a man's soul, I can never change it back again."

"All right," said the boy.

"What are you going to pay me?"

He had nothing but the flute. So the boy gave Habee the flute that he had carved.

Days passed in the city and in the village. The boy's mother searched for him and when she didn't find him, she said, "Alas, he must have fallen asleep at the edge of the river and drowned." They had a funeral and she mourned. "So be it," she said.

Three years passed. During that time, enemies attacked Egypt. The pharaoh lost almost all of his land and half of his wealth. His army was camped in the middle of the desert, about to surrender, when a young man was seen walking alone, across the sand, completely dressed in black. He asked to see the pharaoh.

His presence was startling. He was so handsome and so charismatic that the soldiers brought him instantly before the pharaoh. The Lord of Egypt was impressed himself. And the young man said that his name was the Black Prince. If the pharaoh would let him lead his army, he would win back all of Egypt and land beyond.

The pharaoh agreed. Within weeks, the Black's Prince's strategy won back all of Egypt, lands beyond. He captured more than ten thousand prisoners.

The pharaoh thanked the Black Prince and told him that if he would come to his palace one month from that day, he would reward him. He could ask for power or wealth, he could lead the armies or even share the throne with the pharaoh. The Black Prince bowed and said he would arrive at the palace one month from the day, and walked alone again on foot into the desert.

Word spread about the Black Prince. Women in the kingdom swept clean the streets, scattered flowers in the pathways. On the day of his arrival, the women stood behind trellised windows, watching. Men stood on rooftops. And when the Black Prince walked through the streets, every heart stopped beating. He entered the palace and the court of the pharaoh. He saw the ruler sitting on a gold throne and beside him, on another throne, was his daughter, the Princess Thudmos.

The pharaoh welcomed the Black Prince. He made his offer of power and wealth, of rulership. Without taking his eyes off the princess, the Black Prince said, "I want neither power nor wealth. I ask only for the hand in marriage, of the Princess Thudmos." The princess stood up.

"Father," she said. "If it is your command, I will marry him, but please listen to my story. You see…I was so alone. Every day I sat in my garden. I had no one with whom to talk and share my feelings. Then one day, a boy appeared on the white wall. He didn't notice me. His face was so handsome, like the changing seasons. And he played the flute. Why, he played for the sky and the water, for the beautiful flowers, but everything he played were my feelings. I used to imagine that he would jump down into the garden and that he would love me as much as I loved him. We would spend our days together. And then I would ask him to marry me and he would come and live here in the palace. Then one day, he didn't return. I sent my servants and handmaidens out into the city and into the village. Everyone had heard the boy who played the flute. Then I heard that he had drowned. Father, I know that I can never love as deeply again, and I have sworn that I could marry no one but him."

The Black Prince listened and he looked long at the Princess Thudmos, and then he said, "I once had a love as deep as yours. I would never make you marry me."

And he turned and left the palace. They say that the Black Prince walked back across the desert on foot and was never seen or heard of again.

Learning when to let go is just as hard as holding on, perhaps even more difficult because we still have an emotional connection. Unconditional love by definition means that we will love no matter what others do to themselves, others, or us. This does not mean we have to allow ourselves to be crushed and destroyed. As the giver of love, we have a right to retreat to a safe place for our own emotional and physical well-being. We can offer that love and hold it dear, letting the other know it is there, without being in constant anguish. We can love even if we do not like the other person, but at a safe distance. Once we have made our affection known, we must realize we cannot control the response to it. This is what it means to give unconditionally. Rejection will be less painful if our intentions are good and we are confident of self.

Let us think of ourselves as Sherpas on a long journey, not members of the traveling party. We are the knowledgeable but hired help who have not yet been paid for our services. As guides, we remain at the fringe of the party's internal interactions, yet nearby in case they require our services. When they call us, we are free to move in to guide them. If they wish to be separated from us, we allow that space too. When the journey is finished and our clients are satisfied, we hope they honor their contract and pay us. People enter business deals every day on faith with no guarantees. Why would we expect a loving relationship to be any different? We love on faith alone when we love unconditionally. Part of that commitment is to keep our promises, which means being careful how we make them so that trust remains intact.

Joey and the Kitten

One night, I visited the runaway shelter. My kitten was only four months old and small enough to fit in the palm of my hand. I had taken my dog often and wanted the cat to grow accustomed to taking car trips and visiting other people. I figured she could stay in her carrier if she was too nervous, but I would open the door to see if she would come out and explore. After telling my usual short story, we did some follow up work, I then opened the door to Kashka's carrier.

We had a seventeen-year-old boy named Joey that night. Joey dressed and spoke differently than our city teens, so I suspected he was from someplace else. It turned out he was from New York City and had only been at the shelter a short time. During the entire session, Joey had been disruptive. He pushed all my buttons, interrupted often, and used any number of attention-getting behaviors. He was definitely a Diva Child. The whole time, he kept asking, "When can we see the kitten?" I was a little worried about that. She was so tiny and they were very rough teens that night. Joey did not make me feel any more at ease about it. Still, a promise is a promise.

Kashka surprised me. She came out on her own and walked a few steps from her box. That was when Joey jumped out of his chair and grabbed her. My heart almost stopped beating. I thought, "Oh my God, he's going to kill her." Instead, I learned a huge lesson about teens, promises, trust, and love.

"Be careful, Joey," I said. "She's just a little thing."

"I know, Miss. I have a cat and I miss my cat."

Joey then proceeded to carry the kitten around to every kid and let them each pet her. He amazed me.

Kashka has never gone out with me again, mainly because she's like my other cats. They were all afraid to leave home. I still occasionally took the dog. Doing this let the teens get into my space a little so I could get into theirs. However, maintaining distance is also something I have to do to keep myself physically and emotionally safe. Awareness keeps me safe.

Maintaining Distance

Maintaining distance is not easy for anyone, especially when we care about others. Furthermore, our legal system complicates distancing ourselves from our teens. It determines who is a minor and what services they may receive. When teens are not living at home but legally minors, their parents remain responsible for them even when they are not within family control. Parents may want to step back and allow themselves healing space. However, if their teen commits a crime, gets injured, or is hospitalized, the parents are still legally liable. Reckless behavior can cost parents thousands of dollars, plus personal and family distress. While the system is in place to protect children from abandonment and neglect, little help is available for the family when the child abandons them. Sometimes all we can do is find a place of peace within ourselves or seek support from adult services that understand what we are going through. Caregivers outside the family must also have a support system. We must consider the other partners in the teen-dance including parents, siblings, teachers, peers, and community members. Teens may think they dance alone, but we all participate.

The Butterfly Effect is a theory that says insects fluttering their wings can affect the weather thousands of miles away. This can be said of human relationships too. One person's behavior affects others, even in subtle ways. When working with teens and their "dance partners," we must show compassion and understanding for all those involved, including non-family members and ourselves.

Working with anyone in crisis requires maintaining a safe distance. This is especially true for professional counselors and crisis workers. Distance and a good support system are necessary to avoid transferring trauma. Professionals use several methods to maintain their health when dealing with trauma. Families with at-risk teens can use these also.

I discovered the value of maintaining emotional distance when my niece was pregnant with her second child. She was still single and receiving financial help from the family. My immediate response was judgmental. I was disappointed that she had not learned from her first "mistake." Thinking of it as a mistake was not useful at all in maintaining a working relationship. She needed someone to help her through a difficult time, not to point out the obvious. I suddenly realized I was too close to be objective, so I decided to create a distance between us. She had other supportive friends and family. For my own health, it became necessary to back off. In the end, our family came through it with our relationships intact. I doubt they would have if I had stepped in.

Sometimes we invest so much emotion and time into a relationship that we become attached to the relationship and forget our reason for helping in the first place. Distancing ourselves helps us get in touch with the goal and react with less emotional attachment. Once we have set aside our own expectations and emotional attachment to an outcome, we are ready to enter negotiations.

FOUR PRINCIPLES FOR SUCCESSFUL NEGOTIATION

We have no standard approach to understanding children because they are not average or standard. However, a plan is necessary to achieve the greatest success, assessing each event individually. Waiting until we are in the midst of a crisis is not the time to develop a baseline.

The following four principles for successful negotiation are designed to act as a starting point. They are expectation, judgment, trust/respect, and presentation.

Negotiation is an art. It requires years of learning through experimentation with other people in a variety of situations. Negotiation is an ongoing educational process. We must remain flexible and learn about the specific person or situation. It is best understood through experience, with a willingness to accept occasional failure, remain flexible, and adjust the plan.

We learn the art of negotiation as young children, beginning with our first breath and cry. We discover that the cry initiates a response. We then decide whether we like the response or reject it. Once a child has learned other skills besides crying, such as reaching, making faces, crawling, touching, and eventually language, the child finds new tools for the dance of negotiation. When a response is wanted, a child will continue to use these tools until the response changes to an undesired one. Do we pick him up when he cries? Is that what he wanted? If so, he will stop crying. If not, he will continue and we will dance with him until we find out what is wanted: a diaper changed, a bottle, a pain relieved.

While teens may not cry, they do use other systems to signal that they have a need or want. This is true of all living creatures. It is interesting that there are books on using physical and verbal language with dogs and cats that help us understand them, but we have not really figured out how to talk with our own teens. Teens are the forgotten people. Just because a teen is not telling us their needs, does not mean they do not have them. They most likely are not ready to say anything until it is too late. We must watch for the signals.

I had this experience on an art project with girls at a treatment facility. They were asked to write a story and then illustrate it through collage. When we were finished, I realized some girls had been frustrated and had not understood the project. At the time, I had been unable to offer individual assistance. I explained this to the ones who had the greatest difficulty. One girl made the following comment, which struck me as significant, not just when dealing with this young lady but with youth in general. "As a teen you don't ask for help. If you don't understand it, you just go ahead and do it any way you want."

Teens are a completely unique group of people. While dogs, cats, and other creatures work within a generalized system, human-beings are far more complex. Universal rules do not work with people, yet we expect teens to live by them. How we approach this paradox will affect the outcome of our relationships with them. We do this through the art of negotiation, the foundation for most conflict resolution programs. Resolving conflict is different from *winning* an argument. This brings us to the first and most important principle for success: Expectation

Expectation: Teacher Becomes Student

If we equate success and resolution with getting our way, we are already bound for failure. Entering a battle armed with only the desire to emerge as victor is an approach that sets us up to fail and usually ensures continued conflicts.

"Negotiating hard for your interests, does not mean being closed to the other side's point of view. Quite the contrary. You can hardly expect the other side to listen to your interests and discuss the options you suggest if you don't take their interests into account and show yourself to be open to their suggestions." (Roger Fisher & William L. Ury, *Getting to Yes*, 1981.)

Consider this example: Both parties come to a negotiation with the desire to get what they want, and they want different things. These intended outcomes are opposing each other. We automatically have a no-win situation, unless common ground can be found. The great leaders of the political and business world have long realized that the best outcome is win–win, where both sides get something and both save face. It is perhaps the idea of saving face that is the most difficult in any disagreement, especially between parent and teen. By nature, teens want to exert a certain measure of control. They must do this to enter the adult world. Parents do not wish to lose all control. This is equally necessary if teens are to continue to view their parents as approachable when they need advice. Parents cannot appear weak, not because they need to be the boss, but because the teen needs them to be strong. Would we be more likely to ask a weak, wishy-washy friend for help, or someone who knew what they were talking about and showed the integrity to stand by their ideals? Occasionally a person may want help from someone who will only say yes and agree without conditions. It does not matter if it is good or bad for them. Sometimes even an adult may want to negotiate only if the teen is prepared to do as they ask without question. This has a bandage effect, acting as an immediate fix, but is seldom the most effective. While necessary in a dangerous situation, it seldom makes for a permanent solution. If one negotiator agrees to something under duress, the agreement can break down and return to status quo once the crisis settles. No real change has resulted.

Our expectations going into a negotiation of any kind, will determine the immediate outcome as well as the eventual outcome. Expectations will set the stage for how the entire negotiation takes place.

Are we expecting confrontation from the other party or envisioning a calm respectful discussion of our point of view, *their* point of view, or *all* points of view? Are we thinking that it will fail? Succeed? Have we already called an agency to find the teen a residence before we go into the meeting?

Have we readied their room at home? Who will be disappointed in any of these scenarios?

While we should be prepared and have all the facts we need, we should not assume any outcome until after we have had our initial meeting. Success or failure is determined by expectation.

Going to the table without expectations but with flexibility opens a myriad of possibilities. If we go prepared for a particular outcome, we may have doomed ourselves from the start. At the least, we have not allowed for a variety of ideas. There should be only two expectations taken with us: expect to listen to the other person and expect to think really hard about what they say to us before making a judgment on an action.

The lack of expectation in negotiation is also a form of self-protection and sets the scene for open-mindedness. However, it does not mean we should ignore setting high standards for living. We need reasonable goals for our children's success. How we react when the youth does not meet our expectations is an aspect of unconditional love and judgment.

Judgment

Judgment and expectation are related. If we expect a certain action, reaction, or outcome, we have already passed judgment on the situation. If we have no expectations going in, our judgments will not be based on what we expect but on the facts presented at the negotiation. They will be clearer and more objective. We should remember the vulnerability of teens and their need to exert control. This allows us to be prepared and considerate of their reactions to our suggestions.

For instance, suppose a teen comes to the table expecting us to listen to their ideas and desires. They arrive at the meeting and are informed that we have already purchased new furniture for the spare bedroom and they can come home next week. This sets us up for a potential confrontation. The teen might feel one of three ways. If he was hoping to return home, our thoughtfulness might be satisfying. If the goal was to tell us what he wanted and he perceives that we decided for him, even if we both want the same thing, he might be angry. If coming home was not what the youth wanted, there might be feelings of resentment and betrayal. He came in trusting us to listen and we did. However, he might feel that we have been dishonest in our desire to listen. Relationships are often based on perception.

Adult negotiators may not only expect, but demand an outcome. They may be unwilling to consider another solution, in which case there is no need to negotiate. Adults may not get what they wanted and must be willing to accept that. Sometimes we forget to do this kindness to ourselves and find ourselves extremely disappointed when it does not work out.

Judgment hinders imagination, but it tempers folly. It can save a life, but too much leaves little room for growth. Again, we need to find balance between what we want for our young people and what they want for themselves.

Presentation

In a situation where one negotiator is unwilling to accept anything other than his or her own plan, it becomes a matter of presentation rather than negotiation. We must plead our case, which is not the same as demanding we get our way. It requires a careful study of the "opposition" and planning for all possible events. Teens can benefit from this strategy too, if they wish to apply it to their own negotiations with caregivers. However, most teens do not plan in advance.

When setting up for presentation, it is imperative for an adult not to appear sneaky or suspicious. Otherwise, no matter how much planning went into the meeting, the adult may lose. Trust and respect are keys for success. Teens respect people who do not judge them, but show consideration for their uniqueness. This is not to say that a certain amount of game playing does not take place, it does. Teens will try to shock us. We may impose many rules in our games as adults but the teen game has no rules. They are seemingly created during play and we must somehow learn as we go. This is part of the great experiment of life, where judgment is perceived as a roadblock to progress.

"While we must tread with a certain amount of caution, life requires constant negotiation." (Fisher & Ury, *Getting to Yes*, 1981) This balance between caution and free-fall is exhibited in sparse use of judgment that makes up most friendships. Teens will often respect their friends' opinions more than their families'. Friends will generally accept them the way they are, but the line is drawn at disrespect. If trust and respect are broken, then friendship is broken. In a family, the violator of trust may only continue to receive love and acceptance from a guarded distance. It can take years to find forgiveness when trust is damaged and the bond is undermined.

Another reason many teens seek advice from friends is because their friends will give the advice without passing judgment and will not feel offended if the advice is not taken. This is not so easy for close family members to do. After all, friends have no long-term investment. If a teen fails in his or her quest or gets into serious trouble, the responsibility falls to the parents, both legally and emotionally.

Better results come from leaving judgment out of negotiation and exercising careful consideration. Assumptions lead to disastrous outcomes. We should not set ourselves up for a disappointment and needless internal struggle.

Presenting a flexible package to the youth in a non-threatening, safe environment is more likely to gain us a favorable outcome than a presentation that is one-sided and close-minded.

Trust and Respect

When a teen says, "Wow, you're real," it is a serious compliment. To be real is to be vulnerable, exposed, and trusting of others. Guarded relationships cannot be real. They are masked to avoid emotional upset, thus blocking emotional bonding. Real relationships require risking rejection, being offended, and losing ego, which should not be confused with avoiding emotional abuse. Sometimes remaining distant is a necessary mechanism for protection against the emotional onslaught. To get close to a teen, an adult needs to find that balance between keeping distance and being open and honest.

Teens appreciate trust and respect although they do not always reciprocate. Persistence may be the key to winning those from the teen. Trust and respect are earned. They are not inherent rights and cannot be forced. (See "Star Woman's Basket"_and "Philamondre" found in *Dancing at the Crossroads: Stories and Activities for At-Risk Youth Programs*.)

Usually those who do not like or trust us believe that we have forced our ideas and lifestyles on them. That might include our children, our neighbors, our employees, or just about anyone. If we want to be real and gain success in our relationships, we need to enter them without expectation of an outcome. We must come with open arms, hearts, and minds, and put aside all judgments until both sides have had their say. The gift we give ourselves and our youth is our willingness to listen and respect what they have to say.

> Successful negotiation toward conflict resolution requires change and compromise by everyone involved. During recovery, failing is common for negotiations because the one being treated is a healthier person than the one who did not get the help. We see this in husband/wife relationships during alcohol abuse recovery. There is a greater instance of divorce at these times. A healthy person may not know what to do when they resolve an issue if they focus so much on the other person and their addiction. It can also lead to resentment when one partner receives all the support. Family counseling is very important if we are to have a continuing family relationship as a goal for the young person.
>
> *Diana Koch*

Part III

Journeying Toward an Adult-Youth Partnership

Chapter 4
The Crossroads: Choosing Life's Path

The crossroads is found in Celtic folklore and mythology. Many Celtic stories have elements of in-between places and events, considered neither here nor there and very magical. These crossroads are gateways to the other world, the place of the Fae (Fairy) and the supernatural. Some of these in-between places and events include midnight, the time and space between years, the mists, straddling the land and sea, and sitting on a fence or wall. Even the land itself is between sea and sky.

The teen years are the years between childhood and adulthood. During the teen years, we experience a rebirth. We leave the world of children with some reluctance, as the baby leaves the womb through labor. We come kicking and screaming into the world of adults. Paradoxically, teens thrust themselves into the world of adults when we most wish to keep them in their childhood. The teen years are glorious, frightening, adventurous, dangerous, overwhelming, and chaotic.

The childhood years are timeless, revolving around the child. Adults in a child's life do nearly everything for them. The days of childhood move slowly and seem endless. Time is blurred and the child is oblivious, unable to measure the spaces between events. But time is at a premium for adults. Adults need to order time, carefully weighing and measuring it. Daily life has a planned purpose and we must make sense of chaos and exert our force upon it, bending life to our will. This leads to conflict for adults and teens regarding issues about time.

Movement is another source of relational stress. The teen world is in constant motion; life crashes in on teens like ocean waves. Teens wish to retreat to their child-self world for security and protection, while simultaneously craving to enter into the storm for the sheer love of adventure. The teen world is unique and isolated. Although teens are part of the greater community, they reside metaphorically in that place between worlds. It is a place of multiple contradictions. One can linger there without a need to move forward or back, but is forced to choose a direction at the crossroads where all roads converge. There is no place to go unless one chooses a path.

In Celtic mythology, one may meet the devil at the crossroads. It is a chaotic place. To make the transition from child to adult, one must pass through such a crossroads by way of the teen years. In these years, we learn to negotiate the chaos. Skipping over these years is like taking a journey without sightseeing. We would never discover ourselves. Anything or nothing can happen at the crossroads. All who enter there have equal choices and opportunities, but each road will lead to a different end. Robert Frost said it best in his poem, "The Road Not Taken."

Two Roads diverged in the yellow wood,
And sorry I could not travel both
And be one traveler, long I stood
And looked down one as far as I could
To where it bent in the undergrowth . . .
I shall be telling this with a sigh
Somewhere ages and ages hence
Two roads diverged in a wood, and I –
I took the one less traveled by,
And that has made all the difference.

As in the poem, life has offered us a choice. If we cannot or will not make a choice, it will be thrust on us. Choosing no action whatsoever is to give up control over the outcome. We remain stagnant without choice or movement. Teens decide their life journey at the crossroads. To thrive, they must pass through the crossroads and enter the dance floor.

THE DANCE

Life is a dance. We are in motion from birth to death, to birth again. Each step we take determines our success or failure.

Our young children do not dance alone, instead they stand on top of our feet and we move them about. Adults and children grow accustomed to this symbiotic relationship and depend on its familiarity. As adults, we are reassured of our children's safety by the even pressure of their little feet on ours.

As children enter their teen years, they begin to move away. They create a dance that is unnerving for adults. Unlike ours, the teen-dance is forceful, twisting and turning, and wildly unplanned and unpredictable.

Our adult steps are more evenly spaced, making us uncomfortable watching the teen-dance. Watching them forces us to stand "on the other side," looking back at our own childhood. We recall its difficulties and its lost ecstasy. Teens are not necessarily comfortable either, but comfort is not the purpose of their dance. It shakes loose the skin and allows a new creature to emerge. They must dance with wild abandon and teeter on the edge to prove worthiness of life's next stage.

Sometimes dancers collide. When this happens between a teen and an adult, the adult usually stops dancing, and becomes rigid and immovable. Adults play it safe; security is more important than a passion for adventure. But this is not true for teens. Teens will bounce off rigid adults into uncontrollable movement, not always by choice but out of emotion. This unharnessed energy continues to move until it hits something that pushes back.

Sir Isaac Newton's theory of objects in motion describes the dance of adult and teen. "A body remains in its state of motion unless acted on by an external force. A body acted on by an external force will change its momentum in direction of force, such that the greater the force the greater the change in momentum. Forces always occur in pairs, i.e., for every action there is an equal and opposite reaction."

Teens will continue their uncontrolled behaviors unless we act upon them with some force, in which case their direction will change. Force in this case is meant as a firm hand and an unwavering support that helps the teens make their own choices. Each situation requires separate consideration and some understanding of the individual teen, because force can create movement that leads to an opposite unpredictable direction. If we are not careful, a teen might be pushed farther away, which is not the intent. This dance requires finesse.

The teen years are practice years with a goal to control the movement and learn the right steps. As with all skills and talents, time is needed. Some teens will get it and some will not. Successful youth will learn to flow with the rhythm and create new movements. Those who do not survive will spiral into oblivion, or throw themselves to the ground and never dance again. Our youth need to be taught coping skills.

Coping skills learned in childhood become the tools we use throughout our lives. During the teen years, we recreate ourselves while protecting this new being in several ways. Teens can use the wild dance to keep others away because they are afraid, or may build towers for protection. This is very much like fight or flight responses, skills used instinctively following trauma. To build better working relationships, we need to understand the function of these behaviors and show compassion to our teens.

> The relationship between children and adults needs to be collaborative and based on some fundamental ideas. For someone to relate to children or adolescents, they need to understand development, adolescent growth and critical issues. Adolescence is a time of building identity. The child is breaking away from identification by connection to the family, parents, home, or their siblings and peers. They are trying to establish themselves as separate individuals. Friction between children and their parents exists because there is a change in the relationship. Both parties are trying to let go, causing resistance and confusion. On one hand, family members want things to remain as is; in other ways they want things to change. Staying connected is difficult. During the teen years, children are motivated by a sense

of belonging to a group, which happens to be their peer group. While this might look like extreme behavior to some caregivers it might actually be an attempt to find a sense of belonging. Adolescents are trying to establish themselves as individuals and want to be active with their peer group. Most adolescent peer groups really want to be separate from any other age groups as they go through this growth together.

While there is a sense of an adult/child relationship, we must understand that it houses unique individuals with different behaviors. We should remember that most behaviors serve a purpose. If bad events happen, but there is enough of a connection between the adult and the teen, everybody can take a breath and remember that child's individual needs. The adult can ask, "How does this make sense for this child? What is he or she trying to tell me or express right now?" This is not the same as condoning, excusing, avoiding, or ignoring the behaviors. It is a way of helping an adult deal with hard issues such as drugs, sexual behavior and acting out at home or school. The adult can connect to the "real" child before they address the behavior. This is especially true when working with teens. If we do not honor their separateness as people, they will put up a wall to anything we might have to say, no matter how well meaning that may be. We must accept that it will be stressful for everyone involved, while remembering where the relationship started. We need to remember what the relationship is about and maintain a level of caring, even during those times when we wonder if it is worth it. Difficult times are just one piece of the relationship; they do not define the whole relationship. This recognition helps the bond survive.

Diana Koch

RISKING CONNECTION

When we are injured, emotionally or physically, our natural response is to withdraw. It is a protective measure so we won't be hurt again. But by doing so, we shut ourselves off from what most of us really want; love and compassion. To become connected is a risk. Risk is the only way to obtain love.

Success comes when partners in the dance help each other to thrive. The Inuit story of Skeleton Woman is a good example of how we make each other whole through our compassion. This story may be found as "Dancing in Dark Waters" in the companion book *Dancing at the Crossroads: Stories and Activities for At-Risk Youth Programs.*

Supporting our youth in the most difficult moments can help them "sing" themselves into being. The form they take may not be the one we expect. Nevertheless, we must create a safe place for teens to develop, whether that is the fisherman's warm hut or the stone tower.

> "The first step toward healing in the therapy process is "risking connection." The fisherman's tears represent his ability to risk connection with what he feared. Skeleton Woman was healed through his willingness to be open to the impact she had on him.
>
> We must be present people-oriented beings including all that encompasses: vulnerability, struggle, flaws and mistakes.
>
> At the same time, we need to continue to believe it is worthwhile and relate to each other, whether as clients or therapists. We will then arrive at the place of healing and become safer, happier, and more connected. While relating all our secrets and horrible traumas is not necessary, we need to be willing to get close. It is similar to the difference between having a superficial friend and having a friend we can trust with all our humanness.

One reason the man connected to Skeleton Woman is that he saw her in her humanness. He related to the part of her that mirrored him. They had a commonality in their brokenness. This may be one thing that brought people together after September 11, 2001. We had something in common within that trauma. The blessing of the terrible things that happen to us helps us do difficult things later in our lives. We can learn from them.

Skeleton Woman also teaches us that we can create ourselves. Whether we have been through trauma or not, from the moment we are born we are in the process of recreating ourselves through a constant state of change. The tools we use to help us through this process in life will determine how we change, either positively or negatively. We should surround ourselves with people who see the light in us. We need healthy role models with the skills and wisdom to show us how to interact with others, people who honor us as unique beings. Surrounding ourselves with good mentors, who are engaged in life in a joyful and complete way, helps us effect change on 'self.' Potential is realized without 'shutting down.'"

Diana Koch

Our compassion toward our teens in their "hideousness" helps them bring their true selves to fruition. Supporting our youth in the most difficult moments can help them 'sing' themselves into being. The form they take may not be the one we expect. Nevertheless, we must create a safe place for teens to develop, whether that is the "fisherman's warm hut" or the "stone tower."

Chapter 5
The Metaphor of the Tower

WHAT DOES INSULATION FROM THE OUTSIDE WORLD MEAN to a youth at-risk? One young woman at a residential treatment center had an interesting concept about relationships and how she might view her community's environment. She shared this insight during an activity about destroying the world in our imaginations and putting it back together again. (see *Dancing at the Crossroads: A Guide for Practitioners in At-Risk Youth Programming*)

In the exercise, the teens were asked to choose a superhuman power and one or two realistic personality traits. When asked what she would take out of the world, this young lady's reply to the group was unique. The other girls said they would remove hatred, drugs, alcohol, and prejudice. She said she would remove specific people. This young woman could not specify why she would remove these people except to say that she did not get along with them. When asked what she would put back into the world she said, "People like me, because I would know and like them. I would know their thoughts and read their minds."

In some ways she made me think of the Inuit story Skeleton Woman in which the compassion of the fisherman helps Skeleton Woman recreate herself. The fisherman was trustworthy and equally vulnerable. It takes trust to create a healthy relationship and to allow oneself to be led in "the dance." It takes courage to allow someone else to become part of our personal experience.

A long forgotten misunderstanding destroyed Skeleton Woman, but compassion recreated her. She had to allow herself to become whole again. Many at-risk young women have been abused and recapturing their wholeness is difficult. Instead, they build towers without doors and windows around their hearts. These metaphorical towers are created for protection, but can easily become prisons from which there is no escape. When this happens, the dance stalls until the tower is dismantled or crumbles.

A story that illustrates the building and dismantling of protective towers is the old Germanic tale, "Rapunzel." This is the story of a young girl raised by her witch stepmother, who keeps her captive to protect her from the real world, but the girl discovers the love of a man nonetheless. The witch tries to kill the prince and casts the girl out. The girl and her prince must find each other though neither knows the other still lives.

He is blind and she is the mother of his children, alone and despondent in the world.

Rapunzel

Rapunzel was the result of her mother's desire and her father's choices. When her mother was expecting, the cravings for rampion from the neighbor's garden were so great that she begged her husband to fetch it. When he could no longer resist his wife's pleas, Rapunzel's father climbed the neighbor's garden wall. He pulled a fistful and took it to his wife. She ate it greedily, but was not satisfied.

"More," she demanded. "You must bring me more or I will die."

Again, her husband climbed the wall and stole the neighbor's rampion. This time as he worked his way back home, he found himself face to face with the neighbor who was a witch.

"Are you going so soon, without so much as by your leave?" the old one croaked.

"I am sorry for taking your rampion, but my wife is with child and says she will die without it."

"Your wife will not die but she will have a child, and for stealing you will pay dearly. When your child is born, you will bring her to me."

The man returned to his pregnant wife and gave her the rampion, which she greedily ate. She begged for more and he took as much as his wife wanted, never speaking of the bargain with the witch. When the child was delivered, the husband carried her to his neighbor. His wife screamed for pity, but he would not hear.

The witch took the baby happily and named her Rapunzel, after the lettuce her mother had so desired. She raised the child as her own daughter and Rapunzel loved the only mother she knew.

The old one knew her daughter was beautiful and the men of this world would try to take her. She built a tall tower deep in the forest and when Rapunzel was twelve years old, she locked her precious daughter in that tower. Even then Rapunzel loved the old one, her mother. Every day when the witch came, Rapunzel chose to let her enter.

The witch called,

Rapunzel, Rapunzel
Let down your hair
That I might climb
That golden stair.

The girl's golden hair fell down cascading like water and the witch climbed up. The two spent their days talking of the sights Rapunzel had seen from her window and the lessons of life the old one wished to teach her, but never did she speak of men or sex or babies. They stitched and cooked, and Rapunzel listened to stories. This is how the girl lived and how Rapunzel loved for five years.

At the end of that time, when Rapunzel was seventeen, a king's son happened into the forest. He heard sweet singing in the distance. It drew the prince nearer and nearer to the tower. He desired above all things to enter there, but the prince found no door.

Each day, the prince returned and listened from below her window. Then came a day when he chanced to see the witch approaching. He watched as the old woman stood beneath the tower window and called for her daughter.

Rapunzel, Rapunzel
Let down your hair
That I might climb
that golden stair.

He saw the witch climb up and later down, then walk away into the wood. The prince smiled. The next evening he returned to the tower and disguising his voice he called,

Rapunzel, Rapunzel
Let down your hair
That I might climb
that golden stair.

Rapunzel, delighted to hear her mother, let her hair flow down to the prince. He climbed to the tower window and over the sill. Rapunzel was frightened at first. She had never seen a man before but knew enough to realize this was not her mother. Rapunzel was not prepared for the longing that now moved through her young body.

His words were sweet and soft. The prince reached out a hand to her and Rapunzel felt her face flush at his touch. The young man told her she was beautiful. He said her song had been like the sunshine on his face and cool water on a hot summer day.

The young couple spent long hours together but the prince was always certain to be away before the witch returned in the morning of each day. He always returned at nightfall. Rapunzel trusted him more with every word he spoke and little by little they came closer together. Then, they came together as a man and woman, no longer young and inexperienced. They were in love.

As time passed, Rapunzel's body grew with child. One morning when her mother came to visit, she noticed how Rapunzel's belly bulged and how her daughter's cheeks grew rosy.

"Tell me daughter, how is your appetite?"

"Oh mother, I was hoping you would ask, for these last days I have been ill and cannot eat in the mornings, yet the rest of the day I am ravenous."

The witch now had no doubt what had happened to her dear daughter. Rapunzel was pregnant and some man was the cause. The witch was determined to discover the father. In one quick angry move she struck Rapunzel across the cheek and grabbed her golden hair. With her other hand, the witch used a knife to slice through it.

Rapunzel cried out in astonishment and shame. "Mother! I have done nothing to you. I met a prince and we are in love. Please let me go to him."

"You will go from this place and from my house, but you will never have your prince!"

The witch dragged Rapunzel down a staircase made by spells and conjured a door. Through this she cast Rapunzel and her unborn babes.

"You will wander in the wilderness or die. It matters not to me!"

Their trust was broken and before Rapunzel could speak, she was carried far away, as if on an unseen wind.

As the day wore on, the prince waited and watched for the witch to leave. He did not see her arrive or leave, but he heard his dear love's voice singing in the high tower. The prince stood below and called,

Rapunzel, Rapunzel
Let down your hair
That I might climb
that golden stair.

The witch lowered Rapunzel's beautiful tresses and held them as the prince climbed to the window. When he reached the sill, he found himself face to face with her.

"Your Rapunzel is not here. My daughter is gone and you are alone, dear prince."

The prince lost his balance and his grip as these words struck his heart like daggers. He plummeted down to the forest floor and into thorn bushes that suddenly grew in that place. His eyes were bloodied and scratched by the thorns, and the prince's world went black.

Rapunzel was alone in the world and the desert became her home. Beneath the shade of a mound of stone, the young woman gave birth to twins, a girl and a boy. She wrapped them in what remained of the ragged clothes she wore and fed them mothers' milk. She herself had little enough to eat and it was a troubling time.

For several years the prince walked in darkness, this way and that. One day he wandered into a desert, and in his final despair, thirsty and without hope, the prince fell. He lay there being baked by the hot sun and chilled by the cold night. Then, as luck would have it, Rapunzel found him.

He looked nothing like the prince in his blind and retched state, but Rapunzel knelt beside the man nonetheless. She bathed his face with a dampened scrap of cloth. As she did so, the man's features became clearer. She thought she knew that nose and chin, his form and manner. At last, Rapunzel realized that he was none other than her own beloved prince and tears streamed down her cheeks. Her tears fell into the prince's eyes. As they did, the prince's blindness was relieved and he opened them for the first time in a long time. What a sight it must have been to see the face of his loving Rapunzel. Finding each other again was such a joy. They learned from their troubles, they experienced great happiness, and went on together.

Rapunzel was the result of her mother's desire and her father's choices, but Rapunzel's future was her own.

Unlike the real-life stories of many young people, Rapunzel and her prince lived happily ever after. They probably never worried about money, food, or where they would live. The landlord did not threaten eviction and utility companies did not send bill collectors to their door. However, one can imagine that life would have been easier for them had they been better educated in the biology of life. Sadly, while they had each other, we must assume they had no extended family to lighten their load or help educate their children. In this way, Rapunzel and the prince were probably similar to today's youth. Many young people who choose to have children at an early age struggle more than others, but they come through these struggles. They often work harder and have less than they would have otherwise, but they manage.

CONSTRUCTION: HOW AND WHY TOWERS ARE BUILT

Towers can serve two purposes: they can keep people out or keep people in. Likewise, the architect or builder may be either the resident or someone outside.

The main function of the self-made tower is to keep out the world. The builder creates a safe place for "self" and blocks out anything undesirable. These architects are at a point in life when they no longer wish to be victims. They want to take control. If outward control is not possible, then a safe place to hide or exist must be created. Paradoxically, the builder fights back by protecting self and running. Tower-builders may either leave a chink in the wall in order to see or block themselves in completely. Thus, tower building serves the dual purpose of protection and seclusion.

In the story of Rapunzel, the resident does not build the tower. Someone who wished to keep Rapunzel safe from the world did the building. This tower seems more like a prison than if Rapunzel built it herself, but even a self-made tower can be confining. The difference between self-made and forced confinement is the lack of control the resident has over if and when to leave. With a self-made tower, the resident determines the dismantlement timeline, rather than being forced into someone else's schedule. A forced imprisonment may compel a young person to flee or plot escape, because when something is forbidden it becomes more desirous. It is also true that others outside the tower may be eager to break the defenses and take the resident, as with Rapunzel and her prince. Her isolation, and the prince's desire to obtain the forbidden, created the perfect atmosphere for rebellion.

Dissociation

Sometimes the tower is about dissociating. It represents the disconnection to others and self. Many who have experienced interpersonal trauma use this as a coping skill. They come to believe that they do not have to look outward or inward if the tower has no windows.

Dissociation is "leaving when you cannot leave." When creative resourceful survivors feel pain, fear, brutality, betrayal, or senses their lives are in danger, their only recourse is to use that creative place in the mind that allows them to go away. This experience has been described as watching from a distance.

Children who learn to embellish stories or lie, may be forming a wall to keep themselves at a distance from self and locking others out. When they open the door to being close to others on the outside, the door opens inside. The feelings that rise from this action may be unexpected. The youth may not be prepared to cope. Allowing "presence" can be a frightening prospect, yet healing cannot take place without it.

A trauma takes us away from being present with others and ourselves in different degrees. People who have been through long time trauma, abuse, neglect, or confinement, will frequently have high levels of dissociation that has an addictive quality. We can get in trouble when we believe dissociating is the only way to survive. If so, we will not learn other strategies when they are available. Sometimes, we might dissociate needlessly. Dissociation becomes generalized, and we use it at the slightest bit of anxiety or conflict, boredom, distress or anger. When this happens, we run or hide rather than stay to deal with the situation in other ways.

Diana Koch

Escaping from the Tower

During World War II, some men were in a French prison for many years. Their captors left when France was liberated and all the cell doors were left unlocked. When rescuers searched the prison, they found all the prisoners still in their cells. The captives did not know it was a realistic possibility to leave, because they had adapted to being in captivity as a way of life.

Imprisonment ceased being an out-of-the-ordinary experience. This sometimes happens with trauma survivors.

Stories afford the survivor examples from a distance that are based on emotion and healing. The stories show that people can get away from horrible situations. They can recover the parts of themselves that are healthy. In fact, the survivor will find that she was fine all along. She just lost sight of it. Healing is finding your way home to self.

Diana Koch

The Structure of Confinement

The story of Rapunzel cautions us against rigid confinement. While hers was a physical confinement relating specifically to a male/female relationship, the story is a metaphor for confinement of the spirit.

When we do not validate teen voices and their impending adulthood, we confine their spirits. We must acknowledge their contributions. Confinement stunts growth. Gird a tree and see what happens to it. The trunk will become misshapen and the tree may die. Spiritual confinement leads to resentment and resentment is a staunch tower to breach.

Towers serve the healing process, but self-isolation can lead to depression if we allow it to last too long. Seclusion is healthy in small doses, but self-seclusion can be a sign of self-abuse or suicidal tendency. Furthermore, without mentoring the tower resident may be more easily tempted to follow peers in order to escape.

The first step in the therapeutic process is figuring out exactly how the tower serves a teen. With that information, we can advocate for him or her when the self-made tower begins to come down. Young people need to know there are safe reliable adults supporting them. This does not happen automatically when they choose to dismantle the defenses. This support system needs to be developed over time.

Dismantling the Tower

The safest way to dismantle the tower is by carefully and purposefully taking it down. This requires much planning before the tower-builders even consider taking action. They must be convinced of a good reason to do so and know they have control over the project. They will want freedom to supervise the process and its schedule. Once the builders have accepted the prospect of demolition, they will slowly begin to pull out the stones *they* deem appropriate. At times these builders may replace part of the tower wall and the project will come to a standstill. When this happens, the rest of the caregiver team should allow the builder to determine the best means and time to continue. The project must end and begin at the resident builder's discretion. Successful dismantlement requires a contract prior to the process. Without such an agreement, constant bickering will slow or end it altogether. Controlled demolition takes longer when the builder carefully plans and executes each step. This takes patience, but the results are more permanent and secure.

"Clients need choices in their healing process. Helpers need to be sensitive to potential re-traumatizing when trying to help. How and when the client will heal is a thoughtful process. Listen for the unique signs each client will present regarding how he or she wants to walk in the healing journey. Trauma work, at its best, is a collaborative project. Both the survivor and the healer bring skill and expertise to the journey that are equally valuable to the process," says Diana Koch.

Another way to break down towers is to wait for them to crumble. Accidental demolition risks entrapment and injury by falling metaphorical debris. Even with control, what remains of the tower might not support its own weight and what is left comes crashing down. Destruction may be fast and without notice. If so, the result is violent, placing those inside in danger. Relationships can be irreparably damaged. Assuming a teen is indifferent places our relationship in the path of disaster. Assembling a support team that includes the youth eliminates false assumptions and affords a better chance for success.

Leaving the Tower

"Leaving the tower will require skill and knowledge of how to descend. Clients will need to know where to go when they reach land. This is parallel to initial trauma work, which also requires stabilization and skill-building. For example, before we can learn to scuba-dive, we must learn how to use the equipment, breathe and negotiate the waters. Likewise, survivors need a toolbox of skills to go both safely outside and to their inner places," says Koch.

Creating a Working Demolition Team

Dismantling the tower cannot be done from the outside alone. The outside team and tower resident must work together. In fact, the one inside the tower is the team supervisor who manages the event. This is a difficult notion for some adults. We are not accustomed to giving control to teens. We should remember that the tower serves a purpose. Recognizing and learning to respect that purpose is the first step in bringing the tower down. Knowing the terrain is a step toward reconciliation. An old Irish proverb states, "If you want to know me, come live with me."

The adult team exists to ensure a safe completion of the task, providing a place for the youth to reside once the tower no longer exists. The demolition team should consist of at least one advocate, an adult the teen truly trusts and respects, an adult from whom the teen has "hidden," such as the mother, and a counselor who can help the teen adjust to life on the outside. One person or many may fill these roles. They may or may not include parents or other family members.

This team represents a united front existing solely for the success of the youth. None of the adults on this team should be confrontational; all must be willing negotiators. Team members need to maintain a balance between urgent desire to bring the young person home and non-biased emotional distance. The relationships within the team of youth and adults may ebb and flow between these goals. Balance is healthy for a working relationship. Balance allows neither dominance nor condescension.

Becoming Independent in a Symbiotic Environment

Most teens come through teenhood stronger and wiser, able to meld into adult society. Some are jailed, lost and hopeless, and some end up dead. Well-mentored youth learn to say "no" when faced with decisions that might lead them into trouble, while others follow more destructive paths. Is it their fault when they make bad choices, or is it the result of environmental conditioning? Why do some teens survive experimentation and others do not?

Self-esteem plays an important role in survival and outcome. A youth with poor self-esteem and poor self-confidence may sail through the early years of childhood only to get stuck when they reach Middle School years. The desire to make good decisions may be present, but the teen lacks the belief that he or she can succeed. These youth sometimes seek others who will accept them. This peer acceptance is typically at a level below their own success threshold where they can become the "top dog." These youth adapt to this lower level of thinking and behavior. It is a form of rebellion and they are seeking emotional survival. The desire to fit in becomes a strong drive in their decision-making.

Teens begin to separate from family to become independent, while at the same time they want love and companionship, and they begin to explore forbidden avenues and taboos. This is not thrill-seeking behavior; it is the same kind of exploration infants do when they first learn to crawl. Most youth survive this natural progression from child to adult, but those with weakened self-esteem fall into dissension and eventually may get into trouble.

TABOO

Explorers and adventurers have always been fascinated by taboo. Traveling forbidden paths is the way to discovery. Christopher Columbus sailed waters believed to be treacherous and deadly for anyone who dared take a ship beyond the borders of the known world. Imagine the many things that our society has at its fingertips because people broke taboos. Women wear pants, scientists know how the human body works, astronauts live on space stations. But in breaking these taboos, explorers not only risk their own survival, the existence of all who travel with them is in danger, and therein lies the problem. Society and family members who have experienced life's difficulties, set "taboo-zones" as warnings against folly. Disregarding these signs is risky.

Risk-taking teens are like travelers who read a road sign that says "Danger, Falling Rocks Ahead," then choose to forge ahead anyway, only to be buried beneath those rocks. There is little we can do to stop them, but we can teach our youth what to do if they get buried. A parent may warn a teen that others at a party will offer them alcohol, drugs, or sex. Telling teens to refuse is a good beginning, but teaching them strategies to resist is better. Even when simple solutions, such as walking away or calling a taxi for a ride home are available, they may still say "Yes" because it is easier than arguing or appearing "un-cool."

Children learn to show personal conviction under pressure often long before their teen years. Learning to cope begins on the playground where they set and break taboos experimentally. Children develop superstitions about specific places and items they consider off limits or safe, and form their own taboos. Examples include, "Step on a crack and break your mother's back." or "Home free" in games of tag.

This experimentation is actually practice in preparation for adulthood and its taboos. Children know instinctively that breaking a taboo can be both courageous and foolish. They dare each other to try something dangerous or scary. The beliefs they form about which ones are right or wrong, safe or dangerous will depend on how the dare turns out. It is another way of exploring boundaries.

PLANNING AND PREPARATION

Boundaries are necessary, but throughout history explorers have broken the rules. The difference between safe and reckless exploration is in the planning. A mature explorer creates a conscious calculated plan and has the experiences that allow for coping with unexpected situations as they arise. The new or young explorer has a smaller arsenal of experiences and often lacks a plan. How and why teens enter the "taboo" or "danger zone", and the tools they take with them, will determine their success or failure. Some of this is learned on the playground, but even if the warning is painted in big bold letters, there will be those who interpret taboos as invitations rather than deterrents.

The key to survival is the acquisition of coping skills and lessons learned from mistakes, as well as a strong family or mentor. Coping skills vary and children learn a myriad of techniques from simple rhymes for dealing with liars, cheats, and those who tease them, to knowing whom to call or ask for help in an emergency. Complex skills, including knowing when to fight and when to walk away, are taught by parents, communities, teachers, and peers on the playground.

Child Play

Many lessons are learned through play. Children discover their power over others and their weaknesses. They learn that standing up for their ideals can be painful, but the results are satisfactory, although not always immediate. Through play, children find methods for dealing with bullies and enticing friends. They gather a collection of useful rhymes, such as the following.

"Liar, liar, pants on fire hanging by the telephone wire."

"I am rubber. You are glue. What bounces off me, sticks to you."

"Sticks and stones may break my bones, but names can never hurt me."

"Turn your back and walk away, and live to fight another day."

These superstitions and rhymes may not appeal to adults, but most of us can remember learning them. We may think them nonsensical, but superstitions like these give us control over our environment, especially when we feel we have none. (See "Stamping" on page 122)

THERAPEUTIC STEPS FOR TEACHING COPING SKILLS

by Diana Koch

1. Relationship
   - A. Put the past on the shelf for the meantime. Teenhood is a vulnerable time.

B. Take the time to prove to a young person that you are there because you care. They will challenge it, especially teens who have been taught that caregivers do not care or that some care in unhealthy ways.

C. Healthy relationships happen through validation, honoring, and contracting, an intentional agreement of what will happen, for how long, and with what outcome.

2. Engagement

A. Once you come together to talk about the work that needs to be done, you need to have a sense of who is responsible for which piece. It is a collaborative experience, not just to the benefit of the teaching therapist. The young person must also provide a piece of the puzzle to solve their problem.

B. Honor what the teen brings to the table. If you do not honor his methods of coping before treatment, you will not be able to realistically get him to risk giving up old behaviors to try new ones.

C. Many unknowns exist for children who have been abandoned, traumatized, separated, or disappointed by caregivers. They do not do well with additional unknowns that make them feel helpless and out of control. They have been in those positions and they do not usually want to go back to them.

3. Commitment

A. To learn alternative behaviors, one must take risks. Additionally, therapy is not a straight line. The adolescent may test new skills, but may still revert to the original behavior. Throughout the process, it is a seesaw and balance between honoring them and helping them to move toward other choices. They need to feel safe enough to look at alternatives and experience whatever feelings surface.

This may be one way story helps healing. It plays out the character's actions, reactions, and consequences without the youth having to go through the experience. Story is a wonderful phase-oriented way of getting kids to feel safer. When the listener relates to the character they settle down and become more present with the experience. That is a huge step for traumatized children. Storytelling is a holistic approach that helps the listener take a risk, handling the grief and loss from a safe distance. Stories express moments that define character, moments that define a state of being trapped, challenged, or freed. The story helps listeners internalize the possibility of a solution. They feel safe enough to step closer to their own similar situation.

> *Therapeutic Exercise*: Have the youth imagine they are sitting in the back of a movie theater. Some "clients" can get no closer than standing outside the theater looking at the movie poster. As they move closer to their struggle, they move closer to the screen. *Diana Koch*

Teaching Coping Skills

One of the most powerful tools for learning and teaching coping skills is story. One story that comes to mind is "The Little Engine that Could." It is a favorite among children who constantly face things that seem too big to handle. To an adult, this story may seem trite and simplistic, but the repetitive phrase spoken by the little engine, "I think I can. I think I can," is a memorable phrase. It requires no explanation. Story speaks a common language and stands as its own teacher. Yet, stories need to be entertaining and sometimes touch difficult issues to be relevant.

Another type of story that teaches coping skills is fable. Aesop's fables, "The Boy Who Cried Wolf" and the "Tortoise and the Hare" are favorites among children.

Folktales such as the Russian folktale, "The Turnip" are also good sources for meaningful story. While "The Turnip" is told mostly to very young children, the message that even the smallest voice can make a difference is something at-risk teens like to hear. They feel insignificant and this tale champions their voices. It also teaches that violence, anger, and loud voices are not the only solutions. Another wonderful story, Kathy Caple's "The Biggest Nose," speaks to self-esteem and self-confidence. In this story, a young elephant is teased because of her nose and discovers how special she is because of it. Teens need to hear they are special, not because of their clothing or their friends, but simply because they exist. Validation is very powerful.

GETTING STUCK IN ADOLESCENCE

Human beings get stuck when they do not follow the patterns in life. Movement stops and they stay in one place. Children who get stuck may become adults who have not matured. Although they are not necessarily permanently stuck, it might be like a slow motion replay of a movie, with individuals moving at a fraction of their usual speed, appearing to go nowhere. In addition, some people just "bloom" later than others, so we must be cautious when we diagnose a behavior.

Nevertheless, movement is important, even when slow. If we keep in mind that there are paths or patterns to follow (not always straight), like tracing a line from point A to point B, we will move toward a goal of some kind. As adults, we act as guides or conductors along this line. Our responsibility as conductors is to know how to operate the brakes and track changes to stop or reverse actions. From time to time, everyone needs to rest, regroup, and learn more fully about certain areas in life before moving on. This is especially true for impulsive adolescents. However, landmarks such as the teen years help us grow and permanent stops or skipping over them may lead to later failure. Each stage in life gives us tools we can use to navigate along the journey.

The goal of becoming successful adults is not what drives most teens. They want to be successful teens. Sometimes that means just making it through another day.

For troubled teens, there is a disconnect somewhere in the pattern, as if lines have been erased so they cannot find their way. Children who have been neglected or abused have skipped over the early process of building trusting and respectful relationships with adults. They have not learned the skills of early negotiation, so they get stuck in a form of limbo, left aimlessly floating in their teen years. These teens have generally not experienced positive adult/child interactions and have not figured out how to make it right. They have not learned appropriate coping skills to move on without stumbling. These at-risk teens exhibit immature and childlike behaviors when faced with confrontation or conflict. In addition, they may lack relationships in which others truly listen to what they say. They have bottled up those childhood exploratory energies because the responses when they have come out to play in the world have been negative. These children may become teens who force their will on others violently, angrily, and loudly. Volatile, these youth explode without notice, or when given the rare opportunity to express themselves, do so inappropriately. These teens can also be the ones who become experimental in all the wrong ways, through drugs and sex. They use these behaviors to hide from or escape reality. They explore the taboos because they can.

When a person is held back from the edge too long and finally breaks free, it can be disastrous. In *Women Who Run with the Wolves*, Clarissa Pinkola Estes calls this the 'feral woman.' She speaks about the domesticated woman who becomes free without protective systems in place. This is also true for youth who suddenly discover their freedom when no coping skills are in place.

Adults may find some comfort in keeping children in their childhood, safe and protected. Being stuck in place is safer than running wild, but this may be detrimental to development. Over-protectiveness does not allow children to become whole, thriving, vital, and contributing adults. We cannot follow them through life holding our hands over their heads to keep them from bumping into things. Childhood is a time for learning. Teenhood is for practicing and experimentation, exploration and growth. Sooner or later, an adolescent must become an adult and they can only do this by taking the journey. Hansel and Gretel is a hero's journey story, a metaphoric example of the subtle ways adults become youth role models and how young people cope with danger.

Part IV

Introduction to the Healing Art of Story:

Chapter 6

Using Hansel and Gretel with At-Risk Youth

Hansel and Gretel

The children sat on the steps just outside their woodland home. They heard their parents talking in low whispers.

"We won't have enough to see us through the winter," their father said.

"It's the children. They're getting older and they don't contribute to the house. It's time for them to leave," their mother replied.

The girl was afraid. "Leave home? What would we do? Where would we go?"

"It's okay," said her brother. "Don't be afraid."

The boy was worried too, he just wouldn't say so.

Suddenly the moon, which had been hiding her face behind a cloud, shown down upon the path that led to their home. The little white pebbles that lined the path glowed in the dark. The boy listened to a distant voice, then filled his pockets with the pebbles.

In the morning, their mother rudely awakened the children kicking the bed and shaking them.

"Get up! Get up, lazy children. The sun is already in the sky and we have a long journey today."

She shoved a crust of bread into their hands. "Don't eat it all at once. It must last the day."

Their mother carried a sack and their father had an ax over his shoulder. They led the children deep, deep, deep into the forest.

Occasionally, the boy stopped and looked over his shoulder. Then, he dropped a pebble on the ground. His mother caught him.

"You there," she scolded. "What are you doing? Why do you dawdle?"

"It's just that I thought I saw my little white cat on the roof waving goodbye," he said.

"Nonsense," replied his mother. "It's just the sun glistening off the roof tiles. Now don't dillydally."

Finally, they came to a clearing. The mother pointed to a rock.

"Make a fire, sit, eat your bread and be quiet. Your father and I will return when we are finished."

The children did as they were told. They heard the steady chop, chop, chop of their father's ax as it fell on the wood. Its sound lulled the children to sleep. When they woke, it was very late and dark. They no longer heard the ax and saw their parents nowhere.

"Where is our father? Where is our mother?" the girl cried.

"I don't know," said her brother. "But I have taken care of us. Look."

He pointed to the pebbles he had dropped along the way. They glowed in the moonlight that now filtered through the trees. The pebbles led them home.

When they arrived, their father was glad to see them. Their mother said, "What took you so long? It's late and we have another long journey tomorrow. Go to bed!"

The next day was the same. Their mother rudely woke them. "Get up, get up, get up. The sun is not yet in the sky and we have a long way to go."

She gave them bread crusts. "Don't eat it all at once."

Again, they led their children into the forest. This time the boy dropped bits of his bread upon the ground.

"What are you doing, boy?"

"I thought I saw my little white cat on the roof waving goodbye."

"Phah! You are foolish. Come along," his mother said, as she tromped ahead.

They led the children deeper into the forest today. Deeper than the children had ever gone before, so deep there was no path ahead or behind. They crawled under bushes and brambles.

"There," the mother pointed. "Sit, eat and rest until we return."

The chopping sound of their father's ax again made them sleep, but this time when they woke it was morning.

"Where are our parents?" the girl asked, tears welling in her eyes.

"I don't think they are coming back," her brother said sadly. "But don't worry, I took care of us."

He pointed to where he had dropped the last breadcrumb and saw a bird carry it off in its beak.

"Now what will we do?" the girl cried.

The boy straightened his shoulders. "We will do what we always do. We will find a way."

He took his sister's hand and together they walked the rest of the day. They saw a little white bird and followed it. Finally, it led them to the edge of the forest. Ahead, they heard the sound of trickling water. They found the stream and a bridge that crossed it. On the other side, the children saw a house. It was made completely of gingerbread.

All the desire inside the children welled up. They were so hungry that they did not think about what they were doing. The children raced across the bridge and began to pull the house apart with their hands, stuffing it into their mouths and into their pockets. Yet, for all the food they ate, the children still hungered, for it was not food they needed most. They never gave thought to who might be in the house.

"Nibble, nibble, little mouse. Who's that nibbling on my house?" The voice came from inside.

"It's the wind," the girl answered.

"Wind? I think not," said the voice as the door creaked open. "Children, I see. Where are your parents?"

"We have none," said the boy.

"We are alone," said the girl.

"Alone? Well, I have food and clothes and a soft feather bed. Come in and I will care for you."

The woman looked so kind. She had white hair and a white apron. They followed her into her house. She kept her promise, fed them hot broth, dressed them in clean clothes, and then tucked them into the bed for the night. All night, the children lay in that soft bed of feathers and dreamed of a better tomorrow. Nevertheless, tomorrow dawned no different from any other day.

"Get up, get up, get up, you lazy good for nothing children."

The witch, for that is what she was, grabbed the boy by his collar and dragged him into the yard. She threw him into a cage, slammed the door and locked it. She placed the key around her neck.

"You Girl," she shoved her finger in the girl's chest. "You will cook and you will clean, and you will do as you are told. Do you understand?"

What could the girl say? She only nodded and did as she was told. Each day she did her chores in silence and fed her brother. He set the leftover bones aside and remained imprisoned.

Each morning the old one came and said, "Stick your finger through the bars, so I can see if you are fat."

The boy had grown cleverer on the journey. Instead of his finger, he pushed a chicken bone toward the old witch who felt it saying, "Too thin to eat today."

Every day when the witch felt the bone, she said, "Too thin to eat today." The boy's sister suffered in silence.

Yet it was not long that the old one's patience grew as thin as the bone. She felt what she thought was the boy's finger. "Too thin to eat today, but I will eat you anyway." She turned to his sister. "Stoke the oven girl. I do not like to eat my little boys unless they are well done."

The girl had grown as had her brother. She replied, "I do not know how to stoke a fire."

The witch looked in her face. "You do not know how to stoke a fire? Did your mother teach you nothing?"

Staring blankly, the girl said, "I would not do it as well as you, Old Mother."

"Ah, very well. I will do it myself. Be sure to watch."

The witch bent over and put her head in the oven. She blew on the coals and the fire sprang to life. The girl quickly grabbed the key that dangled from the witch's neck and kicked the old one into the oven. She slammed the oven door and the witch's screams shook the ground and her ashes floated up through the chimney.

The girl ran to the cage and released her brother. They embraced. "Now, what will we do?" she asked, holding his face and looking into his eyes.

"We will find a way," he replied. "But first, let us search the old one's house. Perhaps she has left us something that will help us on our way."

In one corner of one room, the children found a pile of pearls and gems. They filled their pockets with these and walked back to the woods. They walked all the day until they came to a lake. There was no way round it, but a white swan swimming there said, "Get on my back and I will take you across, one at a time."

The boy did as he always did, "You first, Sister."

But his sister had matured on the journey and shook her head, "No Brother, you go first this time. I will be fine."

The swan carried the boy and then the girl across safely. After a short walk, they found the path that led them home.

Nothing had changed in their absence. Their parents were falsely happy to see them and just as poor in pocket and spirit. Only the children had changed, but that was enough.

They had the pearls of knowledge and gems of wisdom from the witch's house. They used what they had learned and took care of themselves.

Stories we typically think of as children's stories are equally suitable for older individuals because they were originally told to entire communities. In ancient societies, everyone gathered to hear stories with little consideration for audience age differences. Children were exposed to more "real" life events, experiencing birth, illness, and death in their homes every day.

A listener will only understand the metaphors in the stories that relate to their own life experiences. For instance, sexual connotations are contained in some stories that young children hear but they do not understand them until they have sexual experience, or have grown up in families that discussed such things openly.

The story of "Little Red Riding Hood," which many theorists consider a story about menstruation and coming of age, is a classic example. For young children, the story is merely a cautionary tale about obeying adults, but for adolescent girls, it might be a story about losing virginity. Likewise, the story of Hansel and Gretel is about defeating a witch, but it can be so much more.

Hansel and Gretel touches on the issue of abandonment that many young children fear and know. The witch is the embodiment of evil for them. Teens have these same fears but they are not likely to listen to a "baby story." When telling this story, consider not using the story title or the names of the children. Teen listeners will get all the way to the place in the story where the children see the house before they realize what they have been hearing. By then, they are hooked. They will want to know how the children survive because they identify with their difficulties. By not naming the characters, teens can more easily place themselves in the story.

Listeners need to know how stories end and want them to end well for the characters. Remember, they identify with the characters. If a character survives, so can they. If the "bad guy" is punished, their real bad guys may receive justice too.

If we do not finish a difficult story or do not allow the characters success in their journey, we leave a big question for younger children in particular. They may be afraid that the witch in Hansel and Gretel is still alive and will come after them. And the truth is, sometimes the characters fail. We can't always candy-coat the truth, but there is always a learned lesson and we must make certain that it is highlighted.

In the story of Hansel and Gretel, the children must destroy the witch. She cannot survive and nobody else can do it for them.

For teens, finishing the story is important because these stories act as models for their own choices. Too many teens have the tendency to start projects and never finish them, many because their lives are disrupted. When story characters complete a task, teens see that it is possible. The story of Hansel and Gretel also opens a discussion on the use of symbols in story. This idea is the foundation for discovering personal myth and a model for writing exercises in the classroom, discussed later in this book.

THE METAPHORS OF HANSEL AND GRETEL

Some people may argue that the story of Hansel and Gretel and many other old fairy tales no longer serve their purpose. Yet they are as relevant as ever because metaphors transcend time and place. Modern media storytelling, television in particular, requires little thought or imagination. We are told what to think and the answers are fed to us. Tales such as Hansel and Gretel do not tell us everything. Instead, the message is revealed through the characters' actions. The answers unfold as the story is told, inspiring independent thought.

Many classic metaphors are present in the story Hansel and Gretel. One example is pairing weak, powerless children with controlling adults. In Hansel, we have a boy who takes care of his sister. In Gretel, we see a girl who does little but cry. We may infer that she is younger and less experienced than the boy. Some will say this is sexist, but this story is the girl's journey more than the boy's. While her brother always has a plan and shows courage, at the end of the story Gretel finds the strength to take care of him.

The father does not play much of a role in the story except to appear weak and henpecked. As with many similar stories, he may be there just to show there are two parents. Metaphorically, the mother is the teacher/nurturer and the father is the provider/disciplinarian. In this case, the father has not provided well for his family. As the mother states, he cannot feed them all.

It is the mother's role to "push the children from the nest." Outwardly the mother, or stepmother in some variations, is cruel. Nevertheless, she does her children a great service by sending them out on their own to grow and mature. Teens who hear this story will most likely have a different opinion about the parents. Many may have been told they are no good, too much trouble, and unwanted. Looking at the parents in the story with a metaphorical lens is for the storyteller to do, not the listener, unless the discussion is part of a follow-up activity on the use of metaphor. The storyteller needs to know the purpose for telling the story, even if the listener gets something totally different from it. Either way, we need to be mindful of both views and the issues that may surface as a result.

Symbolism includes characters as well as numbers, objects, and colors. An abundance of the color white in this story, found in the white cat, the white swan, the moon, and the white bird may all represent hopefulness. In all four cases, the children use that hope to their advantage. They escape punishment by saying they see a cat on the roof and find their way in the dark using the moon. The bird leads them out of the woods, and the children make it across the water on the back of the swan that appears out of nowhere. The use of white pebbles and bread are also representative of this hope and aid. The children were never really alone after all. Hope was their guide and talisman against the darkness.

Koch reminds us that therapists need this hope as well. They must initially hold the hope until the youth is ready to embrace it.

Houses represent security, but the children's house was not secure. Thus, when they saw the gingerbread house they ran to its security and devoured it. These children were hungry. The edible house was not only food for their bellies, but also food for their souls. Yet, deprived of what children desire, they were oblivious to danger. The children forgot they were in a strange place and became greedy. The witch seized her opportunity to ensnare them.

"Children and youth who have a history of being victimized or neglected are at a much greater risk of re-victimization. Offenders report that they look for these vulnerable children, just as the witch found Hansel and Gretel," says Koch.

Witches and aged people in stories are the "wise ones." The stereotypical witch may be offensive to some, but we should not change story elements just to be politically correct. We should do so only if it makes the story stronger and serves the audience. Images of the witch as cruel and ugly are effective. Changing her to a beautiful, kind woman would change the story's meaning. Her persona serves a purpose.

Young people will not always accept the wisdom presented by their adult caregivers. The witch, representing the sum of adult knowledge, must place the characters in difficult situations, then manipulate and direct them covertly toward their goal. She answers their questions and eventually they are led to maturity. She must be fearsome and sometimes ugly so the characters do not wish to linger. They must go on to complete their journey. If the witch had been a kindly lady who gave the children everything, the children would have stayed indefinitely. They would never have matured or grown wiser. The witch had to act worse than their mother. Even the mother had to be cruel or the children would have been stuck in their childhood. The mother is a device to motivate the children to seek their own way.

While we should not kick our children out of the house or threaten to harm them, the stories we tell serve as models for the process of becoming an adult. If our children are nourished with the stories of the world, we may not need to force them to seek their own way.

Before Hansel and Gretel could get to the old woman's cottage, they had to cross a bridge. That bridge represents what separates childhood from adulthood. They literally stand in teenhood when they stand on the bridge. By crossing it, they move to the next phase of growth. In this story, they were reckless, as are many teens in the "real" world.

Deprivation and risk-taking behaviors sometimes follow suffering. At-risk youth often associate with people who meet their needs, whether or not those relationships are healthy. In Hansel and Gretel, the witch's disposition was not the problem. The danger was the children's needs and the capability and availability of the witch to meet them. This may be one reason teens become involved with gangs. A gang meets a need. It offers acceptance, rules, structure, and security.

Young people consider themselves immortal. Death is typically not foremost in their minds, nor do teens typically plan for their future the way adults do. Many teens live for the here and now.

While naivete makes them more courageous, this false sense of immortality makes it easier for youth to engage in dangerous initiations. Some risk-taking activities are benign, such as body demarcation, piercing, and tattooing. While painful, most can be reversed. However, there are more serious and deadly risk-taking behaviors: drugs, unprotected sex, robbery, playing chicken, and Russian roulette. A surprising number of youth die each year from these foolish choices. It is for this reason that elements in a story must be real. In order to reach these risk-taking teens, antagonists in a story must be frightening. The bad guy who represents challenges cannot be weak.

Destroying the witch character is necessary. As previously mentioned, it puts finality to her existence. She cannot come back to hurt the listener later. Imagine her ferocity if the witch had survived Gretel's attempt at destroying her. The children are empowered by bringing about her end. They must be the heroes who overcome adversity if the listener is to believe they can do the same. In this story, the witch's destruction is a catalyst to allow the children to search her home safely, find what they need, and return home. Her ashes do ascend, however, allowing her to come back as the witch in the next story, but for now she is benign.

We may say that witches in all stories are the same character because they represent wisdom. While the listener may not know it and does not need to be told, the witch is the children's teacher. Only a "foolish" child would run headlong into danger, making that mistake again. The unspoken message is a warning to be careful when entering a relationship with someone just because it was easy. The house was tasty, but it was no picnic.

Unfortunately, at-risk youth do tend to make the same mistakes again. This is not necessarily due to stupidity. It is an emotional/biological response. They are drawn to what is familiar and comfortable. This destruction of the witch is a step toward awareness and a reduction of further victimization.

Finally, at the end of the story, Hansel and Gretel cross back over water and reenter their own world. This time, the girl's newly discovered strength and courage lead them. The boy is strong and gains wisdom, as evidenced by his use of the chicken bone. By the end of the tale, however, it is the girl who takes center-stage. She saves her brother, releases him, and has the confidence to let him cross the lake first. She knows she can survive even if the swan abandons her and she is without her brother. Her experience has taught her to become self-sufficient. This is why the story is more *her* hero journey than his. The story is definitely a survival story or hero's journey. It is one worthy of telling to teens, especially those at-risk.

THE RESILIENT CHILD AND SURVIVAL

by Diana Koch

Resilient youth have people who validate them as whole individuals. They are not equated with their situation. These youth often have a skill they can latch onto like art, poetry, sports, or music. These skills enable youth to form identities beyond their trauma and help them survive. In this way, they are not trauma survivors, although they were traumatized. Resiliency also relates to survival.

Another factor is community and other caregivers who reach out to these young people and believe in them. Having this support system helps young people make it through difficult times. In addition, cohesiveness of family is beneficial.

Even children who come from very abusive families can have close family ties. They may have to work through what happened to them, but there are still salvageable parts of that family. Throughout their family experience there can be love and moments of connection. This will help a traumatized youth "make it." However, if the family love was not consistent enough, the trauma can feel even more violating because it sets up distrust.

If teens cannot trust or judge when a relationship is safe, they are not able to adjust their approach to that relationship enough to remain safe. Children from abusive homes learn to read the adult perpetrators in order to stay out of the way when it is dangerous. They cannot do this if the relationships are inconsistent.

As therapists, healers and storytellers, we need to evaluate each child in each situation and not make generalizations. We should never dismiss the value of the family based on what happened, because most of these children will go back to that family. If we do not honor the family as part of the child's life, we cannot really help that child. In some ways, not honoring the family invalidates the child. The younger the child, the more important the family is to his or her well-being.

Another piece of the survivor puzzle is the nature of the trauma. Various factors come into play if trauma took place when a child was young and can determine that child's degree of resiliency. Neglect can lead to neurological damage, physical deficiencies and developmental and learning disabilities. Many children who are developmentally disabled have been abused and have experienced a failure to thrive. They did not get the basic things that children need. They may have had a mother who was using alcohol or drugs while pregnant.

It is also true that youth may be resilient in some situations, but fragile in others. This can be manifested in a youth who has broken places within self, but is outwardly interested in helping others. This strong drive to help others is a diversion from their own problems. These children's real needs are not met when that happens.

Here is a therapeutic exercise that uses imagery to help the client heal "self" before turning to helping others.

Therapeutic Exercise: Have clients imagine walking through their childhood home. They see their child-self sitting on the step crouched up. Have them sit next to this child-self. They begin talking. Youth should pay attention and listen to the child as if the parent to that little part of self. They might ask, "What happened to you?" Once the youth has listened to the story, they will be better equipped to walk back out to the age they are now and do that final piece of caregiving for self. They can tell that child, "I'm so sorry this happened to you. You're safe now. Come with me."

Even those teens who look resilient might have places that need healing. We need to look beyond what is being presented.

Disaster and Resiliency

One thing that is so devastating about disaster is that we are creatures of ritual, comfort, and routine. We lose our sense of who we are when our house is destroyed, we have no food, our ability to stay clean is gone, or when what is familiar is taken away. We do not miss the things, but we miss the structure of life they represent. A favorite poem by William Carlos Williams titled "The Red Wheelbarrow" is a simple statement in four lines of how much we come to depend on the little things in our lives. We are comfortable by seeing the things we expect. Life makes sense.

"Imagine what it is like for the trauma survivor, " says Diana Koch, "especially the children, when even those they love, or on whom they rely, are not there for them. Consistency and trust are key. Some of the least resilient teens come from drug abusing parents. Their world changes from moment to moment, depending on how that parent is feeling and behaving. These teens might exhibit perfectionist behavior because they feel they can avoid having any problems that way. On the other extreme, they may not bother trying to change things because others conditioned them to believe nothing will help. Struggle becomes an entitlement."

Defense of the Abuser

by Diana Koch

We must always honor the mother and the father at the same time we honor the young person's feelings of being hurt by those parents. While honoring the child's origins, we can also focus on a new direction for that youth. The recognition that the parent will always be the parent is central. Children can love the parent-abuser, and at the same time feel bad about the abuse. Sometimes this brings up guilt for the child and they may ignore their feelings. They assume they have to give up their feelings to survive in the relationship. Our job is to help the youth know they can still have their feelings and survive the relationship. Again, an exercise in imagery is helpful for the young client.

Therapeutic Exercise: Teens should imagine they are sitting face to face with their parent. What would they say to them then? No matter what it is, the parent will not be hurt. The parent will just be quiet and listen. The teens can tell the parent what they need and it will not change the relationship. They can also express their feelings to the therapist as if the parent is still present and listening.

Storytellers can benefit from remembering the importance of family too. It is a way of relating to the teens. Sometimes, we are too sensitive about how we portray the parents and stepparents in stories. While we cannot tell the child that their parent is bad, the stories can show it. They also portray the outcomes of those relationships. Youths may not hate their mothers, but they can hate their mother's behaviors. In the story of Hansel and Gretel, the children go back home even though their parents have not changed. The same forgiveness is shown in the story of Philamondre. In the case of story where a parent or parents are destroyed, they represent the action of the perpetrator not the real parent.

THE TRAUMA OF HANSEL AND GRETEL

The creative child understands what they have to say and is able to read the perpetrator. Gretel read the witch and adapted to it. This was how the children gained freedom. They did not work against the perpetrator, but with her.

Many traumatized children give up their ideals to survive. The problem is, they have to heal from that denial of self. For example, they may have been forced to participate in their own abuse, the abuse of other siblings, or their mother. That is a very painful experience.

Reading the perpetrator is a real art. To do so, the child must understand how to connect with the weakness in that person to get free. These children realize skills and talents they did not know they had and find they can survive on their own. They learn that if they go back, they do not have to abandon themselves. They discover they can think and do things inside themselves that cannot be taken away.

Helping youth find skills that will help them when they return to the "broken" family is part of our job as healers and storytellers. We can help them find a sense of belief in themselves. We can help them make good choices that have boundaries and buffers against being absorbed by the toxicity in the home. In this way, they can survive until they can be free of that. We can teach children these skills, although it may be hard for caregivers because we must accept this is the reality for that child. *Diana Koch*

The younger the child, the less likely they are to have a fully developed sense of self. For a child with halted or slowed development due to trauma, this can continue beyond childhood into adulthood. The story of Hansel and Gretel is a good example of children finding what they need to continue healthy lifestyles beyond trauma. Yet, in the story we also see that we sometimes need help to do so.

The following is a role-playing activity using the story characters and a therapist to highlight these developments. This model may be used by storytellers for better understanding of client issues and by counselors in therapeutic settings. As with any treatment, timing is crucial. Not every client will be able to use this model. This work can be difficult and careful monitoring by trained staff is advised. An amount of creativity and imagination are required.

Model for Character Role-Play: Hansel and Gretel

A storyteller and therapist can partner to use storytelling in a variety of ways. Sometimes it is best just to tell a story and follow-up with an activity or discussion. At other times client role-play of story characters can give a deeper insight about why the client follows a particular behavior and a better understanding of the outcomes of those actions. Using the story of Hansel and Gretel, the therapist and the client may both participate in the search for answers. Our model also serves student therapists and gives the experienced therapist and storyteller a different perspective of situations such as those faced by Hansel and Gretel. (The full experimental conversation may be seen in *Dancing at the Crossroads: A Guide for Practitioners in At-Risk Youth Programming*, Appendix VI.)

Diana Koch took the role of therapist and I acted as Hansel and Gretel. For our purpose, we began with a scenario of the children already returned home following their ordeal with the witch. They had discovered that nothing had changed at home and the reality of life within their family remained the same. Hansel and Gretel sensed both good and bad changes in themselves. They struggled to maintain the gifts of the trauma they experienced.

The characters knew that lessons about strength, persistence, and strategy had been learned, but they did not understand how to use those new skills. This left Hansel and Gretel confused and caused additional friction in the home with their parents and each other. Both children had similar experiences with the witch, but different outcomes in their growth.

When they were with the witch they became acutely aware of their need to survive. For the children, living with the witch was no different than living at home. In both environments they needed to find ways to feel less afraid, confused, and defeated.

The experience of returning home did not meet their expectations. The children arrived home with great urgency, expecting safety, something children hope for in their parents. It is our fairy tale ideal of what parents should be for us. We expect them to be good parents, seeing us with pride and love. Participating in this model, we discovered that this is a truth for many of our clients.

Our expected outcome for these children was to help them realize that they *do not* have to be defined by their environments. We wanted the children to know they had developed new skills and show them how to use them. While the children did not have to accept the witch's behavior toward them, they did accept it from their parents. Many actual clients do just this.

We wanted to help Hansel and Gretel discover why they viewed their parents differently from the witch. They had no other place to go, no way to change their situation. This may be a key to why children run away. They find a way to go somewhere else either physically, mentally, or both. When they do, they are successful because they find real or imagined acceptance or escape.

For Hansel and Gretel, their experience was forced on them through abandonment. As a metaphor, their experience was a rite of passage. Growth had to happen or they would not survive. For use in therapy, we viewed the children in this story as trauma survivors.

Therapy takes many weeks or longer. For brevity, we considered three sessions for the children in the story.

1. Introductory session: How we receive the story, normalize, and validate using psycho education, what the therapist's role would be in helping the client, building trust, and getting the basic story from them.
2. Middle of therapeutic treatment: After several sessions and talking about skills, talk about one part of the story as if it were happening again. Help the client work through that process.
3. End of therapy: Explore who the client is now, help them see that healed person, and learn to take care of self. View how they are stronger and realize their talents, how they use the gems of wisdom and pearls of knowledge mentioned in the story.

SUGGESTED ACTIVITY: Have clients alternate taking the role of listener and story character. If working in a group, the clients would return to the larger group and report as listeners what they heard characters say and what they were told by those characters. If working one-on-one with a client, the therapist can take the role of audience to the client.

COLLABORATIVE EXERCISE FOR STORYTELLER AND THERAPIST: The storyteller visits one or more therapy sessions. The therapist would explain that the storyteller is there to help work on what happened to the clients. The teller is going to tell a story and the therapist will help the clients look at that story in a way that may help them feel better.

The storyteller may tell the story all the way through, or stop at places the therapist would like to discuss with the clients. Blanks can be left in the story for the clients to fill. How the story is told will depend on the clients and the situation. The therapist may discuss how the characters felt and let the clients role-play the character to explore how they felt in their trauma, whether they felt angry, afraid, tense, sad, etc.

OUR FINDINGS: The first session consisted of Diana, as therapist, leading the children through their storytelling. Hansel and Gretel, played by myself, explained what happened to them with guiding questions from the therapist. As the leaders of this session, Diana and I experienced firsthand how difficult it is to talk about trauma, especially in a first session. Diana explained that using a game with the children during this first session would help put them at ease. Gaining their trust and helping them feel safe was our main concern.

As the children told their story, we realized that Hansel felt very brave and clever about his actions, and his role as caregiver to his sister. While Gretel sometimes got angry with her brother, she admitted feeling weak and helpless in the beginning. Their intuitive nature and occasional naiveté helped them survive their ordeal. Seeing the glowing pebbles as little light bulbs was quaint and useful.

The therapist in this exercise should echo what the client says, to verify and clarify without planting thoughts. In doing so, the client feels understood. They know someone is truly listening to them, which helps with trust building.

As the children's story progressed, it became evident that Gretel changed. She began to think that it was unnecessary for Hansel to take care of her all the time. She started to imagine ways in which she could help herself. The turning point for Gretel's growth came when the witch locked Hansel away. Finally, she had to care for herself and him. In the end, Gretel was the one to save the day, eventually allowing the swan to carry her brother first. She had control and took the initiative.

We saw the parallel in the characters of Hansel and Gretel and our clients who sometimes experience role changes after their traumas. Hansel believed he lost his purpose when Gretel became stronger and no longer needed him. Part of our job becames helping him find his new role. Even so, Hansel expressed pride in his sister's strength. In this particular role-playing experience, we were able to help the client feel empowered in his new role as an equal to his sister.

Following their trauma, the children experienced trouble sleeping, eating disorders, and flashbacks. They also needed help coming to terms with killing the witch.

Finally, the children discussed their parents. Hansel viewed his father as weak and was determined not to be like him. He also felt that he did not want to be pushy like his mother. Gretel, who had become stronger, felt at ease with her brother caring for her. She sensed this need in him.

Near the end of the session, after the children had told the story and talked a little about what it was like coming home, Diana asked if they were doing well in school, and if they had any friends. The children explained that they were isolated. They then discussed their future plans. Hansel talked about turning sixteen and getting a job so he could leave home and take care of them both.

Diana finished the session by explaining that they had survived something difficult and they had both grown from the experience.

The following bullet points represent the lessons we learned through this process.

- ✦ Role-playing someone else's trauma is difficult. However, the new insight gained was surprising.
- ✦ Even simple children's stories can be powerful. They should not be taken for granted.
- ✦ Both Hansel and Gretel experienced loss. They were not the same people coming out of their ordeal. However, they were able to find missing pieces in each other. It is important to examine all relationships for better understanding of how they reflect on our image of self.
- ✦ Story characters often represent smaller pieces of the whole. In the story of Hansel and Gretel, we are not actually experiencing the journey of a brother/sister or good parent/bad parent. We are looking at the human experience through a microscope and seeing each piece in representative form.
- ✦ The message for a client is that the children survived their transformation. People can do extraordinary things by sheer desperation to save themselves. The cost of that success is to know we have a darker side, which is something we may not wish to know about ourselves.

- Following a trauma, when the calm sets in, the client may question what they had to do to survive. In our activity, Gretel said, "I don't mind that she (*the witch*) died, but I think about killing her." She thought, "I didn't know I could kill anybody. I didn't want to learn that I could." That feeling cannot be unlearned. Somehow, the client must come to terms with that. An internal struggle exists between what we believe is right and what we know is wrong, and what we had to do.
- "All answers are not obvious in the story," says Diana Koch. "For example, in this story we are not told what happens after the children go home. However, many children with similar experiences return to families where nothing has changed in their absence. We do not know much about these story-parents and their motivations, which is another avenue to explore."
- Trauma puts us face to face with every part of self. We are not always prepared to handle all of that at once. For example, Hansel confronted his need to help his sister in order to feel useful. He found that his bravery came from his caregiving. "If he could go to the brave place, he wouldn't be the one to cry." Hansel was left feeling empty when the trauma was over. Fear and hopelessness set in when we are stripped of that which empowers us. This also happens when we are confronted with parts of ourself we do not want to see. For Hansel, this anxiety came from knowing that he was just a step away from being like his father.
- This activity also helps the storyteller find the power in the story and models potential response from the listener.
- Journal writing would be a natural extension of this model. Using Hansel and Gretel, the client would write about what that sense of powerlessness felt like and what it was like to lack safety.
- Exploring different character motivations and story viewpoints leads to new insights.

When using this activity, the storyteller and therapist should keep in mind that different clients will experience different outcomes, which may not look like the ones given in this exercise. The focus should be on the process, not the product of this model. Each client will need individual assistance throughout the process.

Chapter 7
Empowering Youth and Self

THE ROOT WORD OF IMAGINATION IS IMAGE. We often hear people talk about something they may have done that "destroyed their image." Sometimes people say, "We have to keep up our good image."

We can create who we are and choose what we let others see. Belief is a tool for creation of self. We can believe ourselves into being by using our imaginations. This is not to say that there are no outside forces playing into the success or failure of our creation. However, we are in control. As the saying goes, "Imagination is the key to freedom." People with strong imaginations, and the ability to focus attention and energy toward what is desired, have taken the first step toward changing their lives. This might include moving from poverty to financial security, getting a better education, learning a skill, or obtaining a life mate. Of course, society exerts limitations that can make the journey more difficult, but when we can imagine there are possibilities available to us, we can take action. Those who cannot possibly imagine something better, cease to try.

Today's society is filled with things that can stifle the imagination, and we are bombarded with messages telling us we cannot better ourselves without the help of someone or something else. We are told we need wealth or a certain brand item to make it so.

Imagination can be squelched by too much outside influence, such as television (which does all the thinking for us), technology promising to solve all our problems, and and messages convincing us that nothing is possible beyond what we can see and touch. Believing there is no hope or that someone else will dig us out of the hole, teaches us to give up trying on our own. But, put a little fiction in one's life and interesting things happen. If we allow ourselves to let go and believe, we find that solutions are not always in the obvious places. Reading a good book of stories, believing in things that others cannot see, strengthens our imagination and our ability to visualize all options.

This does not mean we should not have an awareness of our limitations and the tools available to us. We use that awareness coupled with imagination to assess what we already know, become comfortable with ourselves, and find creativity someplace in between. These are the lessons of Hansel and Gretel. It required the witch to show them the possibilities and their parents to get the journey started.

We need reality tempered with creativity to solve problems. For example, scientists must be grounded in reality. A firm grasp on reality helps scientists analyze data without prejudice. They believe what they can prove through testing. Yet, scientists also need imagination to conceive possible outcomes of their experiments and form hypotheses.

Many things we take for granted would not exist if people had not imagined them into being. This includes an endless list of inventions such as airplanes, automobiles, telephones, electricity, modern medicine, and even hairstyles and the foods we eat. The thought process begins with a need, but it takes imagination to make things happen. Unlike animals, people can look beyond the moment and its immediacy and believe in what cannot be touched or has never been created. That's a remarkable ability.

Teenagers must be able to use their imaginations to grow beyond the world *we* have created for them. Likewise, adults must allow them that freedom to explore, within safe boundaries, of course. Youth must take life's journey to complete the cycle of maturation. Adults should provide supervision and guidance, but should not give all the answers to the questions that lead to successful living. Each person must discover these for himself. As adults, we might share our personal stories, but we must accept that teens will take from our experiences what they feel is right for them and leave the rest behind.

Our experience-stories highlight safe boundaries without forcing choices. The stories model possibilities, not absolutes. They help us imagine; to imagine is to find freedom of the spirit. Imagination is empowering. (See "Footprints in the Snow"

CHOICE

Empowerment is key for success in life and a tool needed to feel fulfillment. Self-empowerment is not exclusive of the other people in our lives. It is simply the feeling that we have some control. Feeling in control of self helps one become a happier person with stronger interpersonal relationships. To feel in control we must realize that we have a choice, even in seemingly dire situations. It is important not to put the blame on someone else for the choices we make. Doing so, gives them power over us. We must accept that our choices led us to our destination.

Fatalism theologies teach that we choose from a limited number of paths. We can argue that choice is predetermined and that any path could lead to the same conclusion; however, this is not a completely true picture of the life journey. While we may find a pattern present in retrospect, if we happen to vary our direction just one degree, our lives can be remotely different.

Under the Tuscan Sun is a romantic movie in which an unexpected turn of events places a middle-aged woman in Tuscany. She discovers herself and her destiny through "El Signo de Deo," signs from God. The last few lines of the movie sum it up quite well: "Any arbitrary turning along the way, and I would be elsewhere."

Giving others power over us lessens our ability to change. When teens feel they have no choice, they may rebel, exerting their right to choose. Rebellion can lead to violence and frustration. Our job as adults is to offer them "select" opportunities from which to choose, guide them in their decisions, and not control the outcome.

Some teens will listen to our guidance and some will not. We can do little about that, but we can be mindful of the choices we offer and our intentions when offering them. The thoughtful selection of choices offered and the way in which they are presented can guide teens without telling them which choice to make. Remember, we are teaching our youth to become independent. Knowing this can relieve the stress we feel when dealing with rebellious youth. We actually have a great deal of choice but some things are outside our sphere of control. We can control our reactions, the way we approach a situation, and how we deal with our own emotions, but we cannot control what others do.

A group of twelve-year-old students was given a choice of predetermined mottoes for an art project. They were told they could choose one from the teacher's list or one of their own, if appropriate to our activity.

One young student asked if his motto could be "I cheat, I steal, I lie." While it was indeed appropriate to what we were doing, my response was that it might not be the best choice for him. As I looked in his eyes, I added, "You need to decide if it is the right thing to do." I must admit I was surprised when he chose to use the motto even though the look in his eyes said he knew he should not do so. He was obviously testing his classroom teacher and me.

When his teacher scolded him for using the motto, he placed the blame on me saying, "She said it was okay." I was his scapegoat. At this point I reminded him, in front of his teacher, of the correct facts of our conversation. He had been given appropriate choices and advice that he chose not to take. His face reddened as he realized his mistake. No harm was done, and hopefully a lesson was learned.

Most teens appreciate the gift of choice and guidance, which goes a long way toward building trust and respect. Yet choice is not just the road to an outcome, the ultimate goal is to build self-esteem and self-reliance.

Discovering that we have choices may help build self-esteem. Feelings of helplessness lead to despondency and loss of confidence. Some people decide there is no reason to go on living. They feel there is nothing they can do to change their lives. Learning that choice is always available enables hope and eliminates that feeling of weakness.

Look at the example of hostages upon their release and return home. Many methods are used to break their spirits because a broken spirit can be manipulated. The captors attempt to gain control by removing freedom of choice. Many former hostages state that the way they survived these ordeals was by either telling stories about home and loved ones, or refusing to believe they had no choices. That act of refusal was itself a choice. It does not matter if they were successful in their attempts. What is important is maintaining one's personal integrity to ensure dignity. Choosing how to react in a situation where it appears we have no choice is empowering.

Always ask questions before reacting to any situation. Wait. Breathe. In doing so, we afford ourselves the right to choose that reaction. "How will I say this? Why will I say it? Should I say it?"

When we do make the choice, we must also be willing to take responsibility for the results, good or bad. In most cases, outcomes can be reversed, though sometimes it takes more time to undo them than it did to make the mistake in the first place. We just need to remember that it is possible to make amends. Celebrating our successes and accepting our shortcomings empowers us further.

Sometimes, youth will ignore their choices, hand them over to someone else, in order to avoid responsibility, such as the twelve-year-old who blamed someone else for his choice of motto. There are many reasons why people look for scapegoats. Sometimes people are embarrassed by their mistakes. Sometimes they want to avoid punishment or need to save face. But when we give up our responsibility, we also give up the lessons we may have learned from the event. Acceptance may help us avoid making the same mistake again. That is very healthy.

Avoiding responsibility for choice becomes a more serious problem when it leads to lying in order to avoid losing face or being punished. Much to the teacher's credit in the situation with the boy and his choice of motto, she spoke to the student apart from his peers, lessening his embarrassment. Although his actions clearly displeased her, she did not pursue it further. She stated her thoughts and that was the end of it. Hopefully, the student got the message. She knew that harassing him further would not change his future decisions. Only his willingness to accept his mistake and not make the same mistake again would be helpful.

Sometimes we give power to others because we cannot bear being wrong. This might stem from repeated severe punishment when a mistake has negative consequences. Some teens will just refuse to make any choice rather than risk making a wrong one.

How we react when a young person makes a mistake is actually more important than the mistake itself. While we need to teach children and teens healthy, responsible choice-making, we must be careful not to call them names. This damages self-esteem and the results can be devastating to their future well-being and relationships.

I am sorry to say that I have heard some adults call children animals or stupid. I vividly recall hearing a hall monitor in a school where I was working yell at a group of loud fourth and fifth grade students standing in line.

"You're all a bunch of animals! You're animals!"

My niece's physical education coach in middle school thought her attire was inappropriate. Instead of calling her mother or referring her to a female teacher, he told my niece she looked like a cheap slut.

We have no business speaking to young people in this manner. This kind of verbal abuse is more damaging than we may comprehend. For at-risk youth, it only reinforces their low self-esteem.

We can do much better for our young people by modeling our ideas of good behavior, rather than calling them names. Our society is not serving our children or itself very well if we treat teens like anti-humans. The message in this action is that it is better to avoid responsibility, lie, and blame others. The outcome is less painful in the moment. What young person would want to ask advice of an adult or own up to their mistakes after being treated in such a way?

Chapter 8

The Importance of Using Ritual

Storytelling affords many opportunities for ritual. At least two specific rituals should be included in a session. They are an opening and a closing.

Openings and closings create a time and space removed from the rest of the day's experiences. An opening signals the opportunity to start anew, especially valuable when the session is at the end of the day or after another busy activity. It helps listeners focus on the moment. Closings create easy transitioning to the next activity in the day. If for some reason we forget any of the regular rituals we use when working with young people, they will usually remind us.

Structure plays an important role in our lives and in story, something lacking for many at-risk youth. Structure has a stabilizing effect on teens whose lives have been disrupted. Maintaining a ritual helps them gain control over their environments. Even an individual in a detention center or prison can establish some basic personal rituals, such as preparations for meals and bedtime.

RITUAL, RITES, AND INITIATION

Like Dominique in the story of the "Growing Circle," youth are awakened in the night of their adolescence, and whether they come to life with our help or without it determines their later successes. The aunties and grandmothers in the story of the Growing Circle taught Dominique things she could not learn on her own, things that would take her years to understand, but the secret to this story was their willingness to share. Yet, while they secretly invited her to their circle, Dominique had to ask for their stories. In doing so, she told them she was ready to listen. This is very much like the Amish rite of Rumspringa.

During Rumspringa, derived from the Pennsylvania German term for "running around," Amish youth in some sects are allowed to enter the world outside their own in order to experience it for themselves. They are given freedom to choose between baptism within the Amish church or leaving the community. The Amish know that forcing a young person into a life they do not want will result in resentment rather than acceptance. They have confidence that their youth will choose wisely based on upbringing.

Catholics have Confirmation rites, a ceremony when young adults accept and confirm belief and join with their parents in that belief. The Jewish faith has rites of passage that mark various life stages throughout a person's days. Yet, rites of passage were not reserved strictly for religious ceremony in early society. Traditionally, boys were "breeched" in Colonial times, a rite of passage that held popularity until the 1920s. A boy wore a dress until five years of age when he was ceremonially placed in breeches and accepted into his father's care rather than his mother's. Girls and boys entering puberty were introduced into the adult community in a variety of ways from isolation to survival courses.

Today's rites of passage are watered down to the point where their meaning is lost and youth think of them only as a means for leaving the fold of family, rather than taking on the responsibility of family. Youth are left on their own to discover and uncover the secrets of adulthood. Drinking, driving, smoking, voting, joining the military, and yearly birthday celebrations are about all that remain of rituals today, and many of these are no longer reserved for responsible young adults. Being left on their own to grow-up, children seek these gifts of adulthood before they are ready for them.

Rites of passage and the hero's journey are central themes in many healing stories and speak both to the teen and the adult experiencing life transition.

Ritual is used in religious ceremony but we should not relegate it merely to religion. To ritualize is to give purpose to a specific experience, and is self-empowering. This may be as common as how we get up in the morning, how we prepare to drive our cars, how and when we eat, and how we mark each moment of our day. Simple activities such as brushing our teeth can set into motion a series of actions and create awareness. If we somehow forget to do even one task that is normally done in a specific time and a specific way, we can go through the day feeling as if there is something missing.

The rituals themselves are less important than our awareness of them. We must be mindful of the tasks we perform if they are to be relevant. When we become deliberate and take action with awareness we increase our empowerment over our own lives. For instance, if we are aware of how we rise in the morning we may be more thankful for that new morning and approach the day with purpose.

It is possible to take pleasure in the simplest of things. Tying a shoe is meaningful when we learn to notice the color and texture of the lace and the pattern formed when we tie it. We may be reminded of the first time we tied our own shoe.

These daily routines that sometimes feel annoying, as if they slow us down, take on new significance when we are purposeful. We become less anxious and stressed when we learn to see these routines as rituals. Instead of dreading the monotony, we learn to be thankful for the opportunity that has been given us.

Superstitions

Many rituals in our culture feel empowering, though we may not recognize them as such. These rituals are sometimes called superstitions. Knocking on wood is one example. The action does not keep bad things from happening but we become aware of our actions and words when doing so. For example, we might say to a friend while driving, "I haven't had a speeding ticket in a long time." We reach over and tap the wooden paneling. We look at the speedometer and realize we were going just a little too fast. We slow down. Now we are more cognizant of the speed at which we are driving because we do not want to jinx ourselves.

Other forms of empowering ritual or superstitions are rhymes we might use against bullies, such as, "I'm rubber, you're glue. What you say bounces off me and sticks to you." This empowers us to not be offended by what the other person said.

Teens who are nervous about job interviews might "stamp" all the red cars they see on the way to the interview, as long as they are not the ones driving of course.

"Stamping" is a folk belief meaning to sight an object and give it recognition. To stamp red cars when you see them, lick your thumb, press the thumb to the opposite palm, and use your other fist to stamp it into your palm. By doing this teens are given something else to think about rather than how nervous they feel. It creates a new focus, which is a good way to clear the mind in preparation for the next activity.

When we become directly involved with a ritual like this one, we take control of the situation instead of being driven by emotion. We are empowered.

Superstitions should not be written off as nonsense. Although they have no power on their own, the action of participating in them gives them strength for us, not over us.

The Power of Names

Naming ceremonies are powerful common rituals among indigenous peoples and are used in many modern religious rites as well. These may include speaking a child's name during Baptism or issuing a child a new secret or sacred name.

Many cultures have strict regulations regarding the use of names and the naming of children. In some cultures it is forbidden to speak the names of the dead. It is believed that they will return if they hear their names called. In other beliefs, we speak names to honor the dead. We also name our children for beloved family members. Among some Native Americans, no child is given the name of a living person. That name can only be used after the original recipient dies.

Sometimes secret names are given to a child in addition to the birth name. This secret or sacred name holds the true power of the person to whom it is given. It is never revealed or spoken aloud unless in prayer to the Creator, because to know a name is to hold power over the bearer of that name. Names are how our Creator recognizes us.

We are also empowered by knowing the name of that which we fear. If we can place a name on a thing, idea, or person, we can control it to some extent. Naming is a powerful tool for conquering fear and overcoming obstacles. Names are descriptive and embody larger ideas. For example, some believe that we cannot understand the complex idea of God. His name is understood to embody a vast idea that is inexplicable.

To help empower teens over issues that trouble them, we can help them identify and name those things. Using ritual, we can change what teens fear into something they embrace, but first we must help those teens become part of our community. We do this through rites of passage.

RITES OF PASSAGE

The absence of rites of passage is a disservice to us all. We still celebrate some rites in our daily lives, but few people put much thought into them, and they are no longer an integral part of growing up. They have become matter-of-fact and therefore have lost their empowerment for us.

We acknowledge birthdays, weddings, and deaths. We take our first sip of alcohol, learn to smoke cigarettes, have our first sexual encounter, and experience our first kiss. We apply for a driver's license. These were once communal events that were celebrated in some form, but today many youth travel this path alone because we do not take time to guide them. We have forgotten the profound effect these celebrations have on our future.

Unfortunately, our society often ignores two major life passages, puberty and menopause, perhaps because of the stigmas attached to them and our discomfort in discussing them. Both involve sexuality and spirituality. Both are powerful life-altering events that include physical and emotional changes, related in the way they affect the individual.

Consider how closely puberty and menopause are tied with the rites of birth and death. They are both related to fertility, one a time of planting, the other of reaping. Understanding the emotions and physical changes of these phases helps us understand their connection with other rites we celebrate, such as birthdays, weddings, and deaths.

Our modern society does not like to talk about passages that involve sex or death. However, because they are hugely stressful, we must find positive ways to make meaning out of the chaos. Today's youth will find a greater respect for life when we exhibit respect and honor life as a community. We also need to come to a better understanding of how birth and death are interwoven with our everyday lives. The rites of birth and death are celebrations, metaphorically as well as physically. Birthdays and Funerals are rituals.

Birthdays can and should be celebrated more than once a year. Every time we start a new project or make a step in the direction we want to go we are giving birth to new life through creation. The energy we put into an activity and the energies created by our actions are no less important than labor and childbirth. Think about the empowering feeling young people could have if they celebrated each success, instead of stressing each failure.

A goal is a necessary part of the process toward recognizing that a birth has taken place. An actual physical birth, such as having a baby, is something we can see throughout the nine months of carrying. In the end, we have pain and a tangible child as well as an additional physical change in the body. Measuring success for day-to-day accomplishments that may not involve physical pain requires some kind of goal so that we can mark the passage leading up to that success.

One such goal might be to receive good grades in school, but we must be specific. A "good grade" is subjective unless we define it. Instead we need to say we will get an "A," "B," or "C," or achieve a percentage of gain. Now we can see the results of our actions. Helping our children become successful requires us to help them define their goals in measurable ways. The most important reason to celebrate a rite of passage is to recognize and celebrate these defined and specific successes, no matter how large or small.

> When I was growing up, I got "A's" and "B's" on my report cards with little effort. In order to motivate me to work hard, we could not set the goal at a higher grade, there was no higher grade for me to achieve. My motivations had to be more external and emotional. My celebrations centered on the praise I received for my good work. I was happy when my mother hung report cards, papers, and art

> on the refrigerator and when someone took time to listen to my poems or stories. These efforts provided measurable recognition of my success.
>
> *Diana Koch*

If we are celebrating success, the child should be present to see his or her works displayed and hear our praise. Too often we make positive comments in private when the child is not present. As the saying goes, it is best to criticize in private, praise in public.

The celebration needs to be thoughtful, deliberate, and immediate. We live in a society of instant gratification and at-risk youth require instant praise to regain self-confidence. We can be very quick to correct negative behaviors but put off giving praise. It might be better to make praise instantaneous and use the 24-hour rule before admonishing behavior, unless it is dangerous. In doing so, we may find that our children will self-correct, which is favorable over being nagged and more meaningful to them in the long-term. It is also important for teens to learn to praise themselves, but this takes practice and maturity.

When considering rites of passage, we should also realize that rewards are not all that constitute a ceremony. What is celebrated is not the reward itself but the act that led to the reward. The reward is just a ceremonial representation of that act. We should not give rewards without being mindful of the process. For example, being told we are getting a new bike is not enough. The real triumph is the moment the bike is presented with a bright red ribbon and applause from family members. Or perhaps the reward for success is a new puppy. The moment the puppy is released from its carrier into child's arms is priceless. It is not the puppy itself that is the moment of significance, it is the love attached to the reward.

We can also ritualize the action of reward selection. Unfortunately for many young people, and some adults too, the object of reward is considered more valuable than the achievement behind it. It takes practice to make the recognition for our success the moment of celebration.

A birthday party is a good example of how we go through the motions without thinking about the idea behind the celebration. We give birthday parties because of convention, but they should be given with purpose and meaning. Many birthday parties are given to young children or adults at specific stages and have become extreme social events. Socialization is one goal, but what about the real meaning for celebrating another year of life?

There was a time when life was more dangerous due to disease and labor conditions, poor medical care, and poor nutrition. In previous societies people were considered fortunate to live another year, especially children. Parents celebrated the fact that their child lived. Getting older was and still is about more than black balloons. A passage from one cycle, or one year to the next should be met with joy and thanksgiving. In fact, it can be said that all passages are really birth and death cycles: the beginning and end, then rebirth. Nothing ever awakens for us unless something else dies. A new job requires leaving an old one. Taking a step toward being sober requires the death of drunkenness. An "A" on a math test requires us to give up old habits. As we celebrate a birth, we are often coming from a loss. Therefore we also need to acknowledge our losses as well as our gains. Sometimes we need to do that before we truly appreciate what we have gained.

Sample Death/Birth Celebration

There are many ways various cultures mark life passages. Sometimes a candidate must enter the cave. In the absence of a cave, a covering is placed over the head. Some youth are sent into the wilderness with no more than a spear. In many modern cultures we light the candles on a cake. This is a powerful representation as fire is both destructive and creative. The wax is destroyed while heat and light come into being, death and birth tied together.

Using votive candles purchased in plastic cups is a safe and easy way to engage youth in a candle lighting ceremony. (Appendix: Materials Resource List.) Participants should write what they wish to obtain in their lives on the plastic cup with a permanent marker prior to the lighting ceremony. Remind them that short-term goals are more readily obtainable than long-term goals. After the presenter tells a story, each person will extinguish his or her candle. This story should model a character that gives something up to receive something else.

Before the young people blow out their respective candles to celebrate their wishes, remind them that bringing something to themselves requires giving something up. This is birth and death. Have them think about or speak aloud what they will give up to make their wishes come true. Verbalizing our intentions brings them closer to fruition. It shows we have a conviction to make them happen.

Remember to encourage them to share, but never force participants to reveal their desires out loud.

Finally, invite the youth to relight their candles in celebration each time they move toward their goals.

Note: Be certain to check with the facility before lighting fires; you may not be allowed to have an open flame due to fire restrictions. When this is the case, use imaginative fire or LED candles. Remind youth that candle wax can be hot.

Birth and death are united. Celebrating them can have significant impacts on our lives. This idea came to me several years ago when I lost a good friend. The loss was not a physical passing; it was desertion by the friend. This incident was also the first time I realized that death is loss of anything significant and we naturally grieve that loss. Whether it is being fired from a job, loss of a home or a loved one, divorce, rape, or other significant loss, at that precise moment the feelings are real, emotional and physical. We ask many of the same questions as someone who is grieving: why, how, what did we do, could we have changed it? We feel abandoned, lost, alone, and sometimes betrayed.

After my friend and I parted ways, I spent perhaps a year or two in a depressed state. I got a sick feeling in my stomach any time I was reminded of the incident. I suffered nightmares. One day, the idea came to me that the only way to rid myself of this sadness was literally to bury the past, by holding a ritualized funeral for my lost friendship. I finally understood the power of ritual.

When we take the time to create a specific moment for honoring whatever success, failure, sorrow, or joy we might be experiencing, we place it in a time out of time. It becomes a place out of our ordinary existence. It is a bit like putting it under a glass. With ritual we have captured the event and hold it under our control. Once it is under control, we can do whatever we want with it. We can cherish it, consume it, or destroy it.

Funerals are ways in which we honor our cherished ones and celebrate their lives. Burial and consumption are moments of closure. The ritual funeral I gave for my lost friendship was one of the most powerful experiences of my life. Relief was immediate once it was finished.

To create a time and place for my event, I cleared an area in front of the fireplace and prepared a ceremonial funeral pyre. I assembled my materials: one small covered-basket, lighter, a pen, strips of paper. To perform this kind of ceremony it is possible to add actual memorabilia from the relationship as well as representations of actual objects. Be careful not to overload indoor fireplaces. If zoning allows, an outdoor bonfire can be used.

On each strip of paper, I wrote one bad feeling of which I wanted to rid myself (anger, sadness, jealousy, longing, etc.), remaining mindful of each step in the process. (Conscious thought, not actions, creates the empowerment of such a ceremony.)

I placed each strip of paper into the basket and spoke aloud the good, positive, happy feelings I would like to have. It is best to frame these thoughts as positive rather than negative. I also verbalized what might be the positive outcome of the whole experience. The basket was placed on the pyre and a fire started. I watched as the flames consumed my sorrows. The relief was almost immediate.

The realization of what was born that day took years to understand. Everything I am doing in my life right now probably would not have blossomed in what was a stifling dead-end friendship. My current successes were born from releasing the old. What we produce in our lives is always tied to the energy we expend and where we place priority. Change is a good thing most of the time, even if it is painful at first.

Death is the opposite of birth and does not have to be viewed negatively. Think of birth and death as a circle without an end: when one finishes, the other begins immediately. In this way, we can begin to think of birth and death as a cycle and a blessing. Celebrating a death puts it behind us and moves us into the future. It was upon my grandmother's death in the 1980's that I realized the funeral as a celebration for the living, not the dead.

My parents were in South Korea when my grandmother died. My dad was working for his company in Korea at the time she became ill and making the journey home was difficult. When the doctors said they did not expect her to live, my parents began making preparations to return.

I knew my mother would be devastated if she could not see her mother one last time to say goodbye, but other family members from a distant state were eager to proceed with the funeral and return home. A court order allowed us to hold off on the burial for at least the traditional three days afforded by our religion. In the end, I had no qualms that this was the best thing we could have done for our mother.

Until that event, I had always thought of funerals as something the dying wanted. I guessed it might make them feel loved to know they would be remembered. I never imagined it could be so important to the living. I now realize that having a way to honor and celebrate a loved one's life completes the circle and validates that life. Without it, we feel as if there is unfinished business.

Deciding to put things behind us by burying the past is also a form of death. Allowing something to die is to let go of one's ego and gain a consciousness, to be awakened to the present, which is all we really have anyway. In doing this, we are empowered by conscious choice and can create a deliberate celebration or rite of passage for that effort. Something else is born when we celebrate death.

During a birthday party we bury the old self, even the child-self. We can hold some of the qualities of childhood, such as vitality, curiosity and joy, but must move forward or we are stunted and do not reach the pinnacle of all we can become. Some people get stuck because they do not acknowledge this critical passage.

Teens fall between the worlds of childhood and adulthood. A rite of passage is a vehicle that moves them forward. Older societies did not recognize a time between childhood and adulthood, what we call the teen years. Children went through various stages and moved directly into adulthood. Dangerous rites often marked this ritual leap. There was little time for self-centeredness when a community relied on everyone to survive.

Puberty: Coming of Age Ritual

Young people seek other people who have similar experiences. They share various rites of passage together, most often without adult supervision. The results can be disastrous, including violence, pregnancy, incarceration, and death.

Ancient communities separated pubescent youth into groups of men and women where they learned the facts of life through ritualistic enactments and trials. Boys might be sent to survive for several days with little more than a hunting knife. If successful, they were initiated into the circle of men, with all rights and responsibilities accorded a man of that particular group. Girls were young women when they could conceive. This also meant earlier marriages because of shorter life expectancies than we have today.

Improved medical care and prolonged life has presented a new set of problems. We allow and sometimes expect children to remain children as long as possible. The paradox of this is the biological maturation of children has not changed with the perception of when childhood ends and adulthood begins and, in fact, many girls are going into menses at a younger age.

We live in an era of mass communication when children are exposed to mature issues without adult supervision. Children of yesteryear experienced birth, death, sex, and violence on a day-to-day basis, but it was not gratuitous or for the purpose of entertainment. These were part of their everyday existence and survival.

As we work harder to protect our children from these harsh realities, we should not ignore their existence. Doing so places young people in the midst of difficult life choices without guidance and correct knowledge. Pregnancy becomes a status symbol, death something to be feared or ignored, sex has no purpose except to feel good, and violence is entertaining and without consequence. Young people are coming of age before they are equipped with the real knowledge and community support they need to be successful in life.

Pregnancy

The decision to see a pregnancy to term is for many teen mothers a first step toward maturity. They see it as the first time in their lives they have done the right thing. This is not a commentary of life versus abortion but an acknowledgment that these young people *want* ownership for their responsibilities and actions.

Some teen mothers believe that because their child will rely on them and not abandon them, they as parents will find fulfillment. A child will give them the unconditional love they so desire and it may be the first thing they can call their own.

Having a child complicates life, even for older experienced married couples. The complications are double for teens. Passing judgment on whether it is right or wrong for teens to become a parent does not solve the problem, but neither is it empowering for them to have unplanned pregnancies. Empowerment resides in the moment of choice, to give birth or not, to keep the child or give it up for adoption, or to avoid pregnancy in the first place. None of these choices are easy ones but they are still choices. Furthermore, we are not empowered or mature until we can control emotional reaction, until we can proactively think through the solutions and their consequences, and accept them as our own.

We can do things as a society to make transition easier for our young people. We can acknowledge the changes in their physical beings and celebrate them rather than sweeping them under a proverbial rug of the "big talk" or ignoring them altogether. We have a responsibility to our youth to bring them into the fold of the adult community. Our actions and reactions toward teen issues, including sexuality, becomes a model they use in their own decision-making. If we treat these topics as taboos or trivialize them in movies and other media, we create either an over exposure or false societal norms and beliefs. There is a middle ground we can reach if we celebrate the humanism of sexuality through rite of passage. Sex becomes a natural part of life and something reserved for a time when a youth can make a responsible choice as a member of the adult circle, sacred and not part of a pop culture.

Our modern society cannot be expected to allow parents to abandon their children in the wilderness to survive, but we need to find ways to mark natural biological milestones. Stories bridge the gap between ancient methods and modern ideas.

> The role of the storyteller, elder, or grandparent, who were traditionally the storytellers, becomes a core piece of creating community. This is especially true when children are separated from their home community. The act of storytelling becomes an anchor point, and the consistency of the storyteller being there despite what happens creates a bond much like that in the family. Part of healing for anyone, especially children, is connecting the dots and weaving together the pieces of their lives. Storytellers have the ability to bring together wisdom, journey, pain, happiness, family, phases of development, and life lessons in ways that capture the light in those children. Story moments become a place of trance as in good therapy. The storyteller asks people to get on their magic carpet and go on a journey to look at something. The way it is presented invites the listener to do that in an unthreatening way and provides enough safety and containment so they can look at difficult things. If they were not in that journey with the storyteller, these issues might be things they would not wish to face. Doing this work involves timing, reflection, and phrasing. The listener can experience and see things that help them heal and form identity. *Diana Koch*

A deep connection is made when stories are told to troubled teens. For that moment, the only ones in that time and space are the teen and the teller. All doubts, troubles, and fears are forgotten. Things happen to characters, but the listener is safe.

Whether teens are biologically ours, or ours by reason of community, we serve ourselves as well as them when we dance with them, for them, toward them. In the best model of community, we bring our youth from that place of childhood to the crossroads and show them the way to go from there. We form symbiotic partnerships and become their mentors, so that they become the hero's of their own stories.

For more information on working with at-risk youth using story see *Dancing at the Crossroads: A Guide for Practitioners in At-Risk Youth Programming*, and *Dancing at the Crossroads: Stories and Activities for At-Risk Youth Programs*.

Appendix

Materials Resource List

This is a listing with contact informational for materials used in various suggested activities and gifting.

Votive Candles: I purchase mine in bulk from a religious supply company. They come in individual plastic cups, which can be written on, in permanent marker. The brand I order is shipped from the Muench-Kreuzer Candle Company in Syracuse New York. They are called Disposable Votive Candles.

LED Lights: Battery Operated Candles.net
http://www.batteryoperatedcandles.net/CG10280-CH-p-tea-lights.html
Nasco Arts and Crafts 1-800-558-9595 or www.info.nascofa.com
Sax Arts and Crafts 1-800-558-6696 or www.saxarts.com

Fimo Clay: This is pliable clay once you have warmed it up with your hands. It comes in a variety of colors and when baked at approximately 350 degrees for about 15 minutes will become permanently hardened. It is perfect clay for bead making. Fimo clay may be purchased at most art supply stores.

Mask Forms: These are available in a variety of styles but I like the whole mask best. You can also purchase a few items for decorating masks. Also consider flea markets and yard sales as a good source for decorations. Mask forms are white and you may want to spray paint a few in various colors before a session. We have painted them at the session but they take too long to dry.

Colored Sand: You will need to purchase a large quantity of the sand. Begin collecting jars in which to keep it. Jars are easier to use than the little plastic bags the sand is shipped in.

Popsicle or craft sticks: Many arts supply companies will sell these by the box.

Faux Eagle feathers: Any kind of natural feather will work.
http://www.crazycrow.com/turkey-wing-feathers.
Colorful feathers are best for some projects such as mask-making. You can usually find bags of feathers at your local craft store.

Giant Rider-Waite Tarot Deck: a wonderful tarot card for exercises in metaphors and archetypes. You may need to modify the cards for some agencies.
U.S. Games Systems, Inc. Stamford CT 06902

Gemstones, bracelets, tribal stones, and geodes: You will need to buy a large quantity of these products but they will last a long time.
GeoCentral 1-800-231-6083 or www.geocentralonline.com

Oriental Trading Company 1-800-228-2269 or www.orientaltrading.com
Trinkets of all kinds, including small bags of trouble dolls.

Glow-in-the-dark pebbles: A 1 pound bag contains just over 100 pebbles. Their 1" pebble white, glows blue. They also have blue/blue and green/green. About $20 per pound. You can also use ordinary white pebbles found at your local garden supply store.

CORE SYSTEMS P.O. Box 1545, Comox, BC Canada V9M 8A2
Toll-Free 1.855.777.2673 (CORE) or http://www.coregravel.ca/shop/

Bibliography

Bettleheim, B. *The Uses of Enchantment.* New York: Random House. 1976.

Courlander, Harold. "Two Friends: How They Parted." *The King's Drum.* New York: Harcourt, Brace, & World, Inc. 1962.

Cox, Allison & Albert, David H. *The Healing Heart: Families.* Canada: New Society Publishers. 2003. ISBN 0-86571-466-5.

Cox, Allison & Albert, David H. *The Healing Heart: Communities.* Canada: New Society Publishers. 2003. ISBN 0-86571-468-1.

Elder, John & Wong, Hertha D. *Family of Earth & Sky.* Boston: Beacon Press. 1994. ISBN 0-8070-8529-4.

Estes, Clarissa Pinkola. *Women Who Run with the Wolves.* New York: Ballantine. 1995. ISBN 0-345-39681-2.

Fincher, Suzanne F. *Coloring Mandalas.* Boston: Shambhala. 2000. ISBN 1-57062-563-2.

Fisher, R., Ury, W.L. & Patton, B. *Getting to Yes.* Penguin Group. 1981.

Fontana, D. *The Secret Language of Symbols.* San Francisco: Cronicle Books. 1993.

Forest, Heather. *Wisdom Tales From Around the World.* Little Rock: August House. 1996.

Hamilton & Weiss. *Children Tell Stories: Teaching and Using Storytelling in the Classroom.* Katonah, New York: Richard C. Owen Publishers. 2005.

Herman, Judith. *Trauma and Recovery*. Perseus Books. 1992.

Holt, D. & Mooney, B. *Ready-To-Tell Tales*. Little Rock: August House. 1994.

MacDonald, Margaret Read. *Peace Tales*. New Haven: Linnet Books. 1992.

Martin, Rafe. *Rough Face Girl*. Paper Star. 1998.

Mooney, B. & Holt,D. *The Storyteller's Guide*. August House. 1996.

Riordan, James. *The Woman in the Moon*. New York: Dial Books for Young Readers. 1962. ISBN 0-8037-0194-2.

Simms, Laura. *Making Peace*. Chicago: Earwig Recordings.

Simms, Laura. "Boy Who Hid in the King's Heart." Parabola Magazine: Issue on SOUL.

Storytelling in the Classroom. Katonah, New York: Richard C. Owen Publishers. 2005.

Wolkstein, Diane. *The Magic Orange Tree*. New York: Schocken Books. 1997. ISBN 0-8052-1077-6.

Yolan, Jane. *Favorite Folktales from Around the World*. New York: Pantheon Books. 1986.

Video:

Masks from Many Cultures. Crystal Video. 1-800-255-8629, ISBN 1-56290-085-4.

Index

P

R

S

About the Author

Lorna MacDonald Czarnota is an award-winning storyteller and author who has delighted audiences in schools, libraries, festivals and conferences throughout the United States, Canada, and Ireland with traditional and original stories since 1985. Her work features historical presentations, storytelling, writing workshops, and motivational presentations. She specializes in work with at-risk youth, Celtic folklore, and the use of music and song to enhance story. She is the author of *Medieval Tales that Kids Can Read and Tell, Legends, Lore and Secrets of Western New York, Wicked Niagara: the Sinister Side of the Niagara Frontier, Breadline Blue, American and Pioneer Sites of Upstate New York: Westward Trails From Albany to Buffalo* and has stories in other anthologies and magazines.

Lorna holds a Bachelor in Creative Studies for Young Children, a Masters in Special Education, and certification in Trauma Counseling. She is the founder and executive director of Crossroads Story Center, Inc., a not-for-profit for reaching at-risk youth through story.

Lorna began working with at-risk youth in 1994, and continues to run programs in run-away shelters, group homes, treatment centers and other venues. She is a leader in this work within the national and international storytelling community. She has presented at storytelling conferences and festivals throughout the United States. Lorna has also worked with teachers and parents of at-risk youth. In 2004, Lorna presented her work to storytellers in Ireland and worked there with inner-city youth. Her work with at-risk youth has expanded to storytelling with abused women and their children, and communities in disaster. Educators of young children in Blacksburg Virginia, brought Lorna to work with the community at large in April 2007, following the shooting on the Virginia Tech campus. Recognized by her community Lorna is the recipient of the 2006 Oracle Award from the National Storytelling Network, the Hopevale Incorporated Volunteer of the Year Award, Storytelling World Award, and was nominated as a Univera, United Way Community Hero.

www.crossroadsstorycenter.com
www.lornamacdonaldczarnota.com
www.storyhavenstudio.com